Roots of the Republic

ROOTS OF THE REPUBLIC

Dr. Gary D. Hermalyn, Project Editor
Brother C. Edward Quinn, Consulting Editor
Professor Lloyd Ultan, Consulting Editor

Signers of the Declaration of Independence
by Brother C. Edward Quinn

Signers of the Constitution of the United States
by Brother C. Edward Quinn

The First Senate of the United States 1789-1795
by Richard Streb

The First House of Representatives and the Bill of Rights
by George Lankevich

Chief Justices of the United States
by Geroge Lankevich

Presidents of the United States
by Lloyd Ultan

ROOTS OF THE REPUBLIC

THE
PRESIDENTS
OF THE
UNITED STATES

VOLUME 6

Lloyd Ultan

GROLIER EDUCATIONAL
Sherman Turnpike, Danbury, Connecticut

*President portraits, courtesy of The Library of Congress
and The White House*

Published 1996 by Grolier Educational, Danbury, Connecticut
© 1996 by The Bronx County Historical Society

Set ISBN 0-7172-7608-2
Volume ISBN 0-7172-7613-9
Library of Congress number 95-082224

For information, address the publisher:
Grolier Educational, Danbury, Connecticut 06816.

*Cover design by Smart Graphics
Book design by Henry C. Meyer Jr.*

TABLE OF CONTENTS

ACKNOWLEDGMENTS

For encouraging my research endeavors, I must first thank my colleagues at the Edward Williams College of Fairleigh Dickinson University, especially Dean Kenneth Vehrkens. Thanks must also go to Mr. Robert R. Hall and Dr. Gary D. Hermalyn, President and Executive Director, respectively, of The Bronx County Historical Society, who first suggested the need for a book of short character sketches on those who occupied the highest office in the land, and who encouraged me to write one. I also thank the staff of The Society, Ms. Kathleen A. McAuley, Curator, Mrs. Laura Tosi and Ms. Mary Ilario in the Library, and Mrs. Kay Gleeson, Secretary, for their unstinting support. No task was too large or too small to engage their undivided attention when I needed their help. I have to thank Robert DiLallo for his incisive comments on the manuscript. I also must thank my own family for putting up with all the quirks a historian must display while engaging in the detective work of hunting down information and in the hermit-like endeavor of writing. Above all, I must thank Brother C. Edward Quinn of Manhattan College, whose works, *The Signers of the Declaration of Independence* and *The Signers of the Constitution of the United States,* form the best of models for this type of book.

Lloyd Ultan

ABOUT THE AUTHOR

Lloyd Ultan is a Professor of History at Edward Williams College of Fairleigh Dickinson University. He is also the Historian of The Bronx County Historical Society, having previously served for five years as its President. Professor Ultan is the author of several articles and books about the history of The Bronx, including *The Beautiful Bronx (1920 - 1950),* and was the founding editor of *The Bronx County Historical Society Journal.*

INTRODUCTION

The United States functions under a written Constitution formulated by a remarkable group of men who met in Philadelphia during the sweltering summer of 1787. Their production was monumental. Not only did they form a new government on the basis of reconciling their several understandings of history, experience, and theory, but they convinced the people, through elected delegates to state conventions, to ratify the document.

Putting a new government into operation, however, is different from creating one. Words written on parchment, no matter how respected, provide a meager guide for coping with the realities of domestic and foreign issues and of political differences. The system of checks and balances enshrined in the American government, moreover, almost promotes conflict among a two-house body which enacts laws, a President who administers them, and a judicial system which interprets them. The tension existing among these three branches of government forms a major motif in the history of the United States.

Although the framers of the Constitution envisioned the three branches as coequal, it is the presidency that has emerged as the focus of the American governmental system. While it is true that the Congress has substantial powers, and that the Supreme Court, through its decisions, can alter or abolish cherished American institutions or long-established social and economic conditions, the President has a built-in advantage in setting policies and programs. The Congress is a deliberative body chosen from different constituencies, each having its own priorities. No one member of the House of Representatives or the Senate can unilaterally set priorities for the nation. The Supreme Court, although chosen for life, cannot act unless a case is placed before it; and, since it is a multi-headed body, no one Justice can act alone. Only the executive branch is led by one person and elected by a national constituency. The President, by making legislative suggestions to Congress, appealing for national support, and appointing administrators and Federal judges, can indeed set priorities for the entire nation. It is, therefore, no wonder that most American historians tend to divide the country's past by presidential administrations.

It is thus evident that the personality, experience, and philosophy of an incumbent President has much to do with the direction the nation takes in both domestic and foreign affairs. His abilities, both political and administrative, also do much to explain his administration's successes and failures. Therefore, to understand how the provisions of the Constitution were put into effect, and which directions the nation took at various times in its history, attention must be paid to the character and background of each man who became President of the United States.

These character sketches of each of the nation's Presidents are organized chronologically starting with George Washington   and proceeding to Bill Clinton. Grover Cleveland, who had two nonconsecutive terms, is presented only once, since the focus of this volume is upon the person, not the term of office.

In the space of two centuries, the office of President of the United States has become central to governing the country. Through examining those who occupied that office, this volume is an attempt to uncover why this happened.

THE ORIGIN AND DEVELOPMENT OF THE PRESIDENCY

Even before the opening of the Constitutional Convention at Philadelphia in 1787, political philosophers, such as John Locke, had spread the belief that separate legislative, executive, and judicial authorities balancing each other was the best way to prevent a tyrannical government. These ideas were well known to the members of the Convention and, in their debates, they referred to them often. In creating the presidency, the members had recourse also to history. They looked at the powers and limitations of the Archons and Tyrants of the ancient Greek city states, the Consuls of Rome, the medieval Holy Roman Emperor, the more modern Kings of France and England, the elective King of Poland, and the Governors of the thirteen states.

The first mention of a Federal executive in the Convention's deliberations came in the Virginia Plan, largely prepared by James Madison and introduced by Governor Edmund Randolph. Proposed was a paid collective of an unspecified number of men elected by Congress to execute the laws and to meet with a council of judges to exercise a qualified veto on bills. After almost a month deliberating in a Committee of the Whole, the members agreed that there would be a single executive chosen by Congress having the power to veto bills, but who could be overruled by a two-thirds majority of each house of Congress.

After little deliberation, the Convention gave the task of fleshing out the powers of the executive to a Committee of Detail. This committee recommended that the executive be titled President of the United States, be elected by the Congress for seven years, and not be eligible for reelection. He would have the authority to give information to Congress on the state of the Union and to recommend matters for its consideration, to execute the laws, to commission military officers, to receive ambassadors, to correspond with the state Governors, to grant pardons, and to act as Commander-in-Chief of the armed forces. He would also be required to take an oath of office and could be removed by impeachment with trial by the Supreme Court.

The matter of the presidency was not taken up again until the Convention's work was nearly done. A committee of one representative from each state, chaired by David Brearley, considered postponed matters and made its recommendations on the presidency in early September, 1787. The committee established the four-year term, the method of election, the requirement that the President be a native-born American citizen at least 35 years of age, the method of impeachment with trial by the Senate, and such additional authority as the powers to make treaties, to appoint ambassadors, judges, and other officers with Senate consent, and to require written reports from Cabinet members. The President would also have the power to convene extraordinary sessions of Congress or either of its houses, and, in the event of a disagreement over the time of adjournment, to adjourn the Congress to another date. These provisions were approved and became part of the Constitution.

The scope of the substantial powers given the presidency by a group of leaders who had recently fought a war against tyranny is extraordinary. The fear that such powers might lead to a new tyranny was mitigated by the knowledge that George Washington was sure to be the first President and that his character would leave its imprint on that office. Indeed, it did, and the character, personality, and political and diplomatic skill of an incumbent continue to have an impact on the successful exercise of these powers, sometimes for many decades after he leaves office.

Weak or vacillating Presidents, such as Franklin Pierce or James Buchanan, sapped the authority of the presidency. Thomas Jefferson, who tried to persuade individual Congressmen at White House dinners, or Lyndon Johnson, who could relentlessly wear down a recalcitrant Congressman with his argumentation, increased presidential authority. Inept politicians, such as Herbert Hoover, were repudiated by their party or the electorate. Clever political leaders, such as Andrew Jackson and Franklin Roosevelt, could use their overwhelming popularity to get Congress to approve their proposals. Those who adhered too closely to ideological principle, such as John Quincy Adams or Woodrow Wilson, were likely to see their most prized proposals defeated. Presidents with strong personalities, such as Theodore Roosevelt or Harry Truman, could mobilize support for many of their policies, but those who showed a weakness for being led by their own appointees, such as Ulysses S. Grant or Warren Harding, were likely to have their administrations declared failures by history. Sometimes a crisis brings about the best in a President, as the Civil War did to Abraham Lincoln, and sometimes it brings out the worst, as the Watergate scandal did to Richard Nixon. Therefore, no matter what powers the Constitution gives the office, to a large extent, it is the President who shapes and develops the presidency

GEORGE WASHINGTON

February 22, 1732   *December 14, 1799*

President: April 30, 1789 - March 4, 1797

If force of character could shape a country, then the United States was shaped by the character of its first President. From the first, George Washington was held up by his countrymen as the model of selfless patriotism in both war and peace. To the surprise of many, at the conclusion of the Revolution, he resigned his military leadership while he was receiving accolades from a grateful populace, and was being urged by army officers to take a kingly crown to wrest control of the country from an ineffective Congress. This unselfish act brought him worldwide fame. When asked to give up his cherished private life to become a delegate to the Constitutional Convention, for the good of the nation, George Washington reluctantly, and with a feeling of apprehension, answered the call of duty and set out once again from his native Virginia to serve his fellow Americans. Washington was chosen the Convention's presiding officer and, by the force of his character and personality, was able to control a disparate group of talented men from twelve states with differing opinions on how to structure a more effective government.

From the beginning, it was assumed that Washington would be the first President. No one else engendered such universal trust. Everyone, including those who had opposed the adoption of the new Constitution, knew that the country would be safe in his hands.

Washington, however, dreaded the prospect of becoming the nation's first President. Part of the apprehension he felt as he neared New York, the temporary capital, came from knowing that every act he performed in his newly created office would set a precedent. Prior to taking the oath of office before a joint session of both houses of the new Congress, he heard the crowd gathered outside Federal Hall, and appeared on a balcony so the cheering throng could also witness the act. That evening, he attended the first Inaugural Ball.

Washington continued to set precedents throughout his two terms. He invited guests to his parties and did not accept return invitations; he conferred with Cabinet members in person as well as by writing; he stormed out of a Senate session and never returned when it refused to exercise its role of giving its advice and consent about an Indian treaty while he was present; he proclaimed American neutrality in the wars of the French Revolution; he vigorously quashed the anti-tax uprising in western Pennsylvania called the Whiskey Rebellion; and he retired from the presidency after serving two terms. Those who followed Washington in the presidential office used his actions as a guide.

Perhaps the hallmark of Washington's administration was his effort to keep the presidency above party as an institution responsible for the happiness of the nation as a whole, rather than the partisan interests of the few. This, combined with his unselfish patriotism, moral rectitude, integrity, and respect for law and the institutions that make it, also set an example of republican virtue, a standard by which every subsequent President could be measured.

JOHN ADAMS

October 19, 1735   *July 4, 1826*

President: March 4, 1797 - March 4, 1801

Because of his character and the political conditions during his term of office, John Adams's presidency suffers by comparison with Washington's. Yet, for decades, Adams was in the forefront of American political life.

This hardworking and ingenious native of Massachusetts, Harvard graduate, and lawyer, agitated ably for American independence. In the process, he gained a reputation for being obnoxious, testy, contentious, vain, and stubborn. The Continental Congress chose him to help draft the Declaration of Independence, a task left mostly to Thomas Jefferson. He also successfully moved to make George Washington the commander of the Continental Army.   As American Minister to Holland, he secured loans from the stolid Dutch bankers to help finance the Revolution. Yet, his personality offended the French after he was named to the peace commission, and also the British after he became the first American Minister to the Court of St. James. Disparaging remarks he heard in London about American republican institutions prompted him to author a three-volume *Defense of the Constitutions of the United States of America,* which enhanced his reputation back home.

Upon his return home, Adams was elected the first Vice President of the United States. Although chafing at the powerlessness of the job, for eight years as presiding officer of the Senate, he helped establish that body's procedures.

When Washington retired, John Adams felt that he had earned the right to the presidency. He did not engender universal trust, however. Political parties, which had formed because of the French Revolution, differed over the proper American response to the European conflict. They also differed over who should govern America. Adams, who believed the people's representatives should be only "the rich, the well-born, and the able," sided with Alexander Hamilton and the Federalists. Thomas Jefferson's Republicans opposed that view. Adams gained a majority in the Electoral College, but Jefferson had the second highest vote and became his Vice President under the system then in use.

Adams, faced with domestic divisions aggravated by active partisan politics and a European conflict, was tried further by many of his fellow Federalists. Hamilton and his followers demanded an all-out war with France in response to that nation's undeclared war on American shipping. The President preferred to negotiate. Thus, in 1800, the Federalist Party was split, and Adams was denied reelection.

In his last year as President, Adams supervised the move of the capital to the new city of Washington on the Potomac, and he became the first to occupy the structure today known as the White House. He also had the last word against his opponents when, in the waning hours of his presidency, he appointed many of his Federalist followers as judges, including John Marshall as Chief Justice.

Following a reconciliation with Jefferson after both men had retired from public life, perhaps fittingly, both died on the fiftieth anniversary of American independence. Adams had reached the advanced age of 90, the oldest age ever achieved by a President.

THOMAS JEFFERSON

April 13, 1743   *July 4, 1826*

President: March 4, 1801 - March 4, 1809

If ever a Renaissance man occupied the presidency, it was Thomas Jefferson. Musician, scientist, agriculturalist, inventor, architect, philosopher, educator, linguist, author, political leader, diplomat, and statesman, it seemed no endeavor could satiate his ever-inquiring mind. His pursuit of political and intellectual liberty for Americans and all mankind occupied his entire life.

Jefferson's pamphlets against British attempts to tax the colonies had thrust him into a leadership position in the Revolutionary cause, and his forceful arguments and elegant style made him a natural choice to draft the Declaration of Independence. As a legislator in his native Virginia, he successfully abolished the aristocratic landholding system and separated the state from the Anglican Church, but he failed to convince others that schools for the poor, a state library, a state college, and freedom for slaves were needed in a true republic.

After two terms as Virginia's Governor, Jefferson returned to the Congress, where he proposed decimal coinage and the Ordinance of 1787 for governing the Old Northwest Territory. He went to Paris, first to serve on the peace commission, then as American Minister to France before being recalled by Washington to serve as the first Secretary of State.

Clashes in Washington's Cabinet with Secretary of the Treasury Alexander Hamilton led Jefferson to form his Republican Party, which stood for individual liberty, low taxation, and an agricultural society against the "tyranny" of the commercial and mercantile interests. The party tended to favor the republican French during their revolution as opposed to British monarchy. As a result, Jefferson received enough votes in 1797 to become Vice President. He had no impact on John Adams's policies, and he continued to build his party. He received enough votes in the Electoral College for the presidency in 1800, but, under the system then in use, his vice presidential candidate, Aaron Burr, tied him with the same vote. Jefferson needed a 36th-ballot victory over Burr in the House of Representatives to become President.

Determined to be an example of Republican simplicity in the presidency, Jefferson arrived for his inaugural on horseback, greeted diplomats in his houserobe and slippers, and communicated with Congress only in writing, rather than appearing in person in the manner of a British monarch. He doubled the size of the country through the Louisiana Purchase, had it explored and made a claim to part of the Pacific coast through the Lewis and Clark Expedition, and successfully warred on Barbary pirates in the Mediterranean to safeguard American shipping. His imposition of an embargo on trade to prevent American involvement in the Napoleonic Wars, however, brought hardship and opposition.

After his retirement, Jefferson kept his faith in reason and education by remaining active as President of the American Philosophical Society in Philadelphia, by founding and designing the buildings for the University of Virginia, and by donating his books to restock the Library of Congress after it was burned in the War of 1812. He died on the same day as John Adams, the fiftieth anniversary of the Declaration of Independence.

JAMES MADISON

March 26, 1751   *June 28, 1836*

President: March 4, 1809 - March 4, 1817

Short, scholarly, and soft-spoken, James Madison, in another age, might have made an excellent college professor. The turmoil of his times, however, thrust this man with a brilliant intellect into politics and swept him into the presidency. This scion of the Virginia planter class received his education at the College of New Jersey, today's Princeton University, graduating in 1771. Soon, he began to draw upon his exceptional knowledge of constitutional law, for he helped draft his state's new constitution, and as a member of the Federal Convention of 1787, became a major influence in designing the structure of the new national government. He then joined Alexander Hamilton and John Jay in writing *The Federalist Papers,* a series of newspaper essays urging people to accept the new document. As a member of the House of Representatives in the first Congress under the new Constitution, he introduced the amendments which became the Bill of Rights.

Despite agreeing with Alexander Hamilton on the desirability of a stronger national government, Madison passionately believed that no one, especially the rulers, had the right to control a man's thought. Thus, his views were closer to those of Jefferson, and he became his able lieutenant in the House of Representatives as leader of the Republicans. When Jefferson became President, in 1801, Madison was named his Secretary of State and, later, the choice to succeed him in the presidency.

Although Madison was an intelligent and thoughtful man, as President, he did not have the political leadership ability to deal with such strong-willed Congressmen as Henry Clay. He also lacked great administrative talents and the ability to inspire people with enthusiasm for his ideas. One of his major personal assets was his wife, Dolley, whose lively personality and beauty graced the capital city's social life.

Moreover, Madison's presidency was plagued by the continued dangers to American shipping and commerce on the high seas in the wake of the Napoleonic Wars, and by the rise of new rambunctious Congressmen from the states west of the Alleghenies demanding further expansion of the country through war. The result was the War of 1812 against Great Britain, a conflict the peace-loving President had tried to avoid.

The war did not go well for the United States. A British force even invaded and set fire to the capital city. The arrival of a signed peace treaty declaring the war a draw, just after Andrew Jackson's remarkable victory over the British at New Orleans, saved Madison's popularity.

The blackening caused by the fires of war necessitated recoloring of the presidential home in gleaming white paint, thus giving it its permanent name, the White House. It also produced a patriotic poem based on the defense of Fort McHenry near Baltimore. Set to the music of an English drinking song, it became the anthem, "The Star Spangled Banner." Thus, the difficult presidency of the scholarly James Madison has left us two continuing legacies, both stemming, oddly enough, from a war he did not want.

JAMES MONROE

April 28, 1758   *July 4, 1831*

President: March 4, 1817 - March 4, 1825

James Monroe's presidency was a time filled with troubles, and yet, it is called "The Era of Good Feelings." Obviously, this energetic, but somewhat shy and very kindly man, could discipline and pacify strong-willed political leaders, and guide the nation through some of the most perilous situations it ever faced, while retaining the deep respect of his close associates.

Glimpses of his character can be discerned in his career before his election as President. At the age of eighteen, he left his studies at William and Mary College in his native Virginia to fight in the Revolution. Before the final battle, he began a three-year period studying law with Thomas Jefferson. This relationship grew into a politically valuable close association. In his last year of study,

Monroe was elected to the Virginia Legislature, and then to the Continental Congress. Believing that the newly written Federal Constitution encroached upon states' rights, he opposed it. Nevertheless, he was elected by the Legislature to the United States Senate in 1790, where he served four years attacking Federalist programs.

Monroe abandoned partisan politics in 1794 when Washington named him Minster to France for two years. Following his recall, he served as Governor of Virginia for three years, whereupon his friend, President Jefferson, sent him back to France to assist in negotiating the Louisiana Purchase, and then across the Channel to be Minister to Britain. Monroe's friendship with Jefferson and his foreign policy experience made him the natural choice to be President Madison's Secretary of State in 1811. From 1814 to 1815, he also acted as Secretary of War because the incumbent was both incompetent and of dubious loyalty.

Thus, Monroe became the choice to succeed Madison in the presidency. His years in that office were marked by the demise of the Federalist Party, leading to the President's reelection in 1820 with the votes of all but one member of the Electoral College. The lack of effective party opposition, however, led to the emergence of a handful of regional leaders, each with a significant coterie of followers, all jockeying for political advancement. The President was successful in keeping them in check, especially during the crisis over the extension of slavery into the territories, which broke out in 1820, leading to the Missouri Compromise, and during the furor caused by Andrew Jackson's hanging of British subjects in Florida on a military expedition against the Seminole Indians across the international border.

The President's name is forever associated with two other events which happened during his tenure. First, the American Colonization Society created Liberia in Africa in 1817 as a refuge for freed American slaves, and its capital city was named Monrovia in his honor. Second, threatening moves in 1823 by European powers to recover the newly-independent Latin American Republics for Spain, coupled with a similar threat by Russia on the Pacific Coast, led to the Monroe Doctrine, a foreign policy statement that was to be followed by succeeding Presidents for more than a century.

JOHN QUINCY ADAMS

July 11, 1767   *February 23, 1848*

President: March 4, 1825 - March 4, 1829

John Quincy Adams, the eldest son of John Adams, could be as irascible and harsh as his father, but he was more often austere and reserved. He was principled and courageous, but the barbs of his political opponents hurt him deeply. Intelligent and experienced in domestic and foreign affairs, he should have been a more successful President, but events were to make his career before and after his term of office more noteworthy.

John Quincy Adams accompanied his father to Europe in 1778 and began his higher education in Paris at age eleven, later enrolling at the University of Leiden, and finally graduating back home from Harvard in 1787. While practicing law in Boston, he wrote a series of essays which led to President Washington appointing him Minister to the Netherlands in 1794. His father later named him Minister to Prussia, and he served there until Jefferson became President. In 1803, he was elected Senator from Massachusetts as a Federalist, but deserted that party in 1807 when it became clear that his views were closer to Jefferson's. He failed to be reelected, however.

After some time teaching rhetoric and oratory at Harvard, Adams was tapped by President Madison to be Minister to Russia, then chief of the peace commission to negotiate the end to the War of 1812, and finally, Minister to Britain. His steadfastness in pursuing American interests abroad made him the natural choice to be President Monroe's Secretary of State. In that capacity, he secured Florida from Spain and drafted the Monroe Doctrine.

Since his two predecessors served as Secretary of State before assuming the presidency, it seemed that Adams was the proper choice to follow Monroe into the White House. With party organizations in flux, however, several candidates appeared. While Andrew Jackson, the nation's military hero, had received most of the popular vote in those states which permitted it, no one received a majority in the Electoral College, thus thrusting the choice on the House of Representatives. Henry Clay, another candidate, then backed the Secretary of State, and the House, on the first ballot, chose Adams. When Clay was subsequently named Secretary of State, thus symbolically placing him in presidential succession, Jackson and his followers charged a corrupt bargain had been made to put Adams in the White House. The continual opposition of Jackson's followers doomed Adams's policies. Perhaps the only joys the president had were his daily early morning nude swims in the Potomac and the nightly diary entries in which he excoriated his opponents.

Following his ineffectual presidency, Adams was elected and reelected to the House of Representatives from Massachusetts as long as he lived. There, he forcefully opposed the extension of slavery and the Mexican War, and vigorously upheld the right of petition against a House rule prohibiting the reading of communications opposed to slavery, thus earning the nickname "Old Man Eloquent." His voice was stilled by a stroke he suffered while on the House floor. The meeting was quickly adjourned as he was carried into the Speaker's Room, where he died two days later.

ANDREW JACKSON

March 15, 1767   *June 8, 1845*

President: March 4, 1829 - March 4, 1837

Andrew Jackson was the most popular president elected in the nineteenth century. Not only was he a national hero for his victory at the Battle of New Orleans in 1815, but he symbolized and fought for the aspirations of increasingly politically conscious frontiersmen, small farmers, and urban skilled workmen. The adoring crowd that followed "Old Hickory" to the White House after his inauguration at the Capitol, and barged into the mansion for a rowdy party, began the tradition of the inaugural parade.

Dignified and courteous, Jackson could also be self-willed and capricious. He relied for advice upon a few personal and political friends outside Cabinet meetings, the so-called Kitchen Cabinet. Because the vast majority of Electoral College members were now elected by the people, rather than selected by State Legislators, Jackson maintained that he had, in fact, been popularly elected. He then claimed that, unlike the members of Congress who represented states or small districts, he was the only public official who represented all citizens. He reinforced that claim when he accepted the nomination of his party's first national political convention, in contrast to his predecessors who were nominated by small groups of political leaders in the states or in Congress. He thus felt free to veto bills merely because he disagreed with their provisions, unlike his predecessors who used the veto only if they considered a bill unconstitutional.

Jackson, also unlike the Presidents before him, did not have a Virginia planter or Massachusetts legal background. He was born in the Carolina backwoods, fought as a young teenager in the Revolution, educated himself, and moved to Tennessee, where he built his home, The Hermitage. He was elected Tennessee's first Congressman when it became a state, and subsequently represented it in the Senate. He also served on the state Supreme Court and headed the militia against the Creek Indians before accepting appointment as a U.S. Army General. His action against the British at New Orleans and the Seminoles in Florida made him widely popular and a candidate for the presidency in 1824. For four years after John Quincy Adams was elected, he charged that there was a "corrupt bargain," a tactic that led to Jackson's successful election on the Democratic-Republican ticket in 1828.

As President, Jackson stood up to the efforts of John C. Calhoun to have South Carolina nullify a Federal tariff, vetoed the rechartering of the Bank of the United States, deposited federal money in state banks, demanded that only gold and silver be used to pay for the purchase of public lands, and returned a federal surplus to the states. In his view, the expulsion of the Cherokees from their Georgia lands to a site beyond the Mississippi, the so-called "Trail of Tears," was an act to preserve the Indians' culture from the corrupt influence of frontier settlers.

When Andrew Jackson left the presidency, he not only had strengthened it as an institution, he had changed its character. The President was now more than just a chief executive; he was a leader.

MARTIN VAN BUREN

December 5, 1782   *July 24, 1862*

President: March 4, 1837 - March 4, 1841

Usually not thought of as a setter of precedents, Martin Van Buren had a number of "firsts." He was the first man born as an American citizen (after the adoption of the Declaration of Independence) to be elected to the presidency, as well as the first man from New York State to hold that office. In addition, Van Buren, unlike those who came before him, was not primarily a planter or a practicing lawyer, but the first professional politician to become the nation's chief executive. Although this son of farmers from Kinderhook in upstate New York was trained as a lawyer, his passion was politics, and, for much of his life, he earned his living holding political office.

Van Buren first held office as Surrogate of his native Columbia

County, was subsequently elected to the State Senate, and later appointed State Attorney General. A political coalition he formed in 1820 with William Marcy, called the "Albany Regency" by its foes, was able to dominate New York State politics for a generation. As a leader of this machine, Van Buren's influence radiated not only throughout the state, but into national politics as well.

The State Legislature elected Van Buren to the United States Senate, where he served from 1821 to 1828, supporting Jackson's claims to the presidency. In 1828, he was elected Governor of New York, but resigned in the following year to become President Jackson's Secretary of State. Through his charm, wit, and enigmatic political skill, which gave him the name of "The Little Magician," he emerged as the president's most influential advisor. Following an aborted appointment as Minister to Britain, Van Buren was elected Jackson's Vice President in his second term, and was thus in position to be the national hero's successor.

With Jackson's blessing, Van Buren won election to the presidency handily, but was immediately faced with the Panic of 1837, an economic depression brought on by Jackson's financial policies designed to halt wildcat speculation. Acting the statesman, Van Buren supported the establishment of an independent Treasury and opposed Federal aid to weak businesses. This policy, however, split the Democratic Party and contributed to the President's defeat for reelection in 1840.

Following his defeat, Van Buren remained politically prominent, and even tried to recapture the presidency. He was denied his party's nomination in 1848 because he opposed the annexation of Texas as a slave state. Within New York, he helped organize an antislavery faction, which eventually became part of the new Free Soil Party, and he was named its standard-bearer in 1848.

Yet, for all his political moves and statesmanship, Martin Van Buren is primarily remembered today for one of the possible origins for the phrase "O.K." There is speculation that it stands for "Old Kinderhook," the place of his birth, used in "Vote O.K.," one of his campaign slogans.

WILLIAM HENRY HARRISON

February 9, 1773   *April 4, 1841*

President: March 4, 1841 - April 4, 1841

The most notable event in the presidency of William Henry Harrison was its ending. Harrison was the first President to die in office, and he did so after a mere 31 days on the job, a victim of freak weather and advanced age. The 68-year old man was inaugurated at an outdoor ceremony on the coldest March 4th in the memory of living man. As a result, he caught pneumonia, and all efforts of his attending physicians failed to save him.

Although his presidency was short, Harrison did make a mark upon history and the mode of presidential election. Born in Virginia, he attended Hampton-Sydney College there. He intended to become a physician, but had to end his studies at Philadelphia in 1791 upon the death of his father, Benjamin Harrison, a signer of the Declaration of Independence. He joined the army to fight the Indians in the Northwest Territory, and his experiences there attracted him to that land. He became the Secretary of the territorial government, and in 1798, was chosen by its residents as their non-voting delegate to Congress. After aiding in the formation of the Ohio and Indiana Territories out of the Old Northwest, he served as Governor of the Indiana Territory from 1800 to 1812.

As Governor, Harrison aggressively pursued President Jefferson's policy of removing the native Indians by any means to open the land for settlement from the East. This brought about conflict with Tecumseh, Chief of the Shawnees, who had welded an alliance of many tribes to oppose that policy. In 1811, at the head of the army, Governor Harrison defeated the Shawnees at the Battle of Tippecanoe, in which the chief's brother, The Prophet, was killed. After Tecumseh joined the British in the War of 1812, now General Harrison defeated a combined British-Indian force at the Battle of the Thames, where Tecumseh was slain. The two battles made Harrison a national military hero.

Politically a supporter of Henry Clay, Harrison served in the House of Representatives from Indiana from 1816 to 1819, and was then elected to the Senate in 1825. In the confused political picture, he was one of the candidates for the presidency in 1836 opposed to Van Buren. To the surprise of the others, he managed to gather the highest vote among them, and this encouraged Daniel Webster to convince the new Whig Party to make Harrison its standard-bearer for 1840.

The presidential election of 1840 turned out to be a carnival. Instead of an exploration of the issues and a partisan, but reasoned, debate among the supporters of the candidates, for the first time, hoopla was resorted to. The campaign slogan, "Tippecanoe and Tyler Too," was used to depict the nominee as a rugged frontiersman teamed with his loyal running mate. When Van Buren's Democrats derisively called Harrison the log cabin and hard cider candidate, the Whigs made the log cabin their symbol and served hard cider at election rallies. The hoopla worked, and Harrison was elected by a large Electoral College majority, but by a narrow majority in the popular vote. Unfortunately, he did not live long enough to enjoy his mandate.

JOHN TYLER

March 29, 1790   *January 18, 1862*

President: April 4, 1841 - March 4, 1845

No one intended John Tyler to be President of the United States. He was obstinate and narrow-minded. A combination of circumstances, however, elevated him to the high office.

Tyler, a Virginian born and bred, graduated from William and Mary College and studied law under his father just before his parent was elected Governor of Virginia. Young Tyler was an avid states' rights advocate, and, as such, served in the State Legislature and the House of Representatives before becoming Governor in his own right from 1825 to 1827.

As United States Senator from Virginia from 1827 to 1836, he opposed President Jackson's fiscal policies and his handling of South Carolina's attempt to assert states' rights through nullification of Federal laws. He thus joined those who opposed Jackson in the Whig Party. That party consisted of those who preferred to see the Federal government pay for the building of roads and canals and for protecting the nation's young industries with the tariff. It also attracted those, like Tyler, who believed in states' rights. Since the two positions were fundamentally incompatible, the Whig ticket in 1840 was a compromise. William Henry Harrison, who followed Henry Clay's ideas of greater government spending for internal improvements and protection of industry, was the nominee for President, while Tyler, a strict states' rights man, was chosen the vice presidential candidate. The hoopla of the log cabin and hard cider campaign helped paper over these differences.

When President Harrison succumbed to pneumonia only 31 days after his inaugural, John Tyler became the first Vice President to assume the presidential duties. The question remained, was he the President or only Acting President; should he take the presidential oath or not? While Congress was debating the issue, Tyler took the oath in the White House, thus deciding once and for all that a Vice President succeeding to the presidency becomes the President with all his powers, dignities, and responsibilities.

As President, Tyler signed a law which gave frontier squatters on public land the right to buy the property at favorable rates before it was auctioned. The final boundaries between Canada and Maine were also established. His veto of a bill favored by Henry Clay to recharter a national bank, however, disrupted the Whig Party. Tyler ultimately led the states' rights advocates back towards the Democrats, and one of his final acts was to sign the controversial bill admitting Texas into the Union as a slave state.

Tyler retired after his presidency until events prompted his return to public life to preside at an unsuccessful conference in Washington in 1861 to avert civil war. Ever true to his states' rights principles, he served as a member of the Provisional Congress of the Confederacy, and was elected to the Confederate Congress, but died before it met.

JAMES KNOX POLK

November 2, 1795   *June 15, 1849*

President: March 4, 1845 - March 4, 1849

James K. Polk is probably the least known great President in the history of the United States. In modern terms, he was a workaholic – in his four-year presidency, he left Washington for only four weeks. Polk matched his work habits with determination and tenaciousness in achieving his goals, and it seemed as if he never smiled.

Born in North Carolina, Polk moved with his family westward to Tennessee, but returned to graduate from the University of North Carolina in 1818. He came home to Tennessee to practice law, and was elected to the House of Representatives, where he was ultimately elevated to the office of Speaker from 1835 to 1839. As such, he was recognized as one of the national leaders of the

Democratic Party. He then returned home to serve as Governor of Tennesee for two years.

At the Democratic National Convention in 1844, there was a decided sentiment for westward expansion, but the question of the annexation of Texas injected the divisive issue of slavery into the debate. Ex-President Van Buren wanted the nomination, but his opposition to Texas annexation roused the ire of John C. Calhoun and the southerners. The deadlocked convention then turned unexpectedly to Polk as its candidate, and made him the nominee. Polk thus became the first "dark horse" to run for President. News of his nomination was also the first to be transmitted by telegraph.

In the campaign, the Democrats imitated the hoopla used by the Whigs only four years earlier, dubbing Polk "Young Hickory" to connect him to the still-popular Andrew Jackson, and distributing hickory brooms with which to "polk" Whig candidate, Henry Clay. The antislavery Liberty Party, however, drew enough votes away from Clay in western New York State to insure Polk's narrow victory.

As President, Polk picked a distinguished Cabinet, but kept his own counsel and set his own policy. He announced that he wished to reestablish an independent Treasury, to reduce tariffs, to adjust the Oregon boundary with Canada, and to acquire western territory. In four years, he accomplished all four of these goals. The last one, however, was achieved only through the Mexican War, provoked when the President sent a military force under General Zachary Taylor into an area where American boundary claims were disputed by Mexico. Except for Jefferson, Polk added more territory to the country than any other President up to that time. The United States had become a continent in size and extended from the Atlantic to the Pacific Oceans.

Despite his accomplishments, Polk was sufficiently astute to realize that he could not win reelection. The opposition provoked by his successful policies was too great and the likelihood of the Whigs choosing the popular General Taylor as their candidate seemed to bode a repetition of the election of 1840. Polk thus refused to run and forbade any of his Cabinet to campaign as well. He died a few months after leaving the presidency.

ZACHARY TAYLOR

November 24, 1784   *July 9, 1850*

President: March 4, 1849 - July 9, 1850

Zachary Taylor was a plain, honest, and uncomplicated man. These assets in his personality, however, were less decisive than his military record in meriting him consideration for the nation's highest office.

Taylor was born in western Virginia and was raised in Kentucky. In 1808, he was commissioned in the army and began a forty-year military career. He fought in the Black Hawk War in Illinois from 1832 to 1833, and in the Seminole Wars in Florida in 1837. It was in Florida that he received his nickname, "Old Rough and Ready" for his simple dress and speech combined with his attention to military preparation for combat. He served as commander of the army's Florida Department from 1838 to 1840.

In 1845, President Polk appointed him to command the army at the Texas border and ordered him to occupy a position between the Nueces and Rio Grande Rivers claimed by both Mexico and the United States. Hostile fire on his position began the Mexican War, which lasted from 1846 to 1848. Taylor won victories at Palo Alto and Resaca de la Palma and then occupied Monterrey. For these, he was raised to the rank of Major General. Later, he led his outnumbered troops in the Battle of Buena Vista against Santa Anna in 1847, and won a resounding victory. This made him a national hero and the presidential candidate of the Whig Party in 1848.

Despite his status as a national hero and his appealing personal qualities, Taylor had no political experience. He had been elected to no local, state, or national office, and was unsophisticated politically. In fact, he had never voted in a presidential election. Nevertheless, the fact that he held no outspoken political views was an asset at a time when almost every public issue, especially slavery, was dividing the country. Taylor, who had settled in Louisiana, owned a plantation there, and as a slaveowner, was regarded by the southern Whigs as one of themselves. In reality, he opposed the idea of secession and did not see slavery as a vital question.

Taylor won election with a small majority of the popular vote. As President, he was guided by his more politically experienced friend, William H. Seward. Taylor's views, unexpected as they were to the southern Whigs, soon lost him support, and his lack of experience placed him at a disadvantage in dealing with Congress. Nevertheless, he injected himself into the debate on the question of the extension of slavery into the territories, making it quite clear that he wished to have California admitted as a free state.

On July 4, 1850, President Taylor attended the ceremony laying the cornerstone of the Washington Monument. Under a broiling sun, he calmly listened to hours of oratory, then returned to the White House where he slaked his burning thirst by eating cherries and gulping down iced drinks. He quickly developed "cholera morbus," probably gastroenteritis, from which he died five days later, only sixteen months after entering office.

MILLARD FILLMORE

January 7, 1800   *March 8, 1874*

President: July 9, 1850 - March 4, 1853

The name of Millard Fillmore has become a byword for obscurity. Modern comedians use his name to provoke a laugh, and a small society has mounted a tongue-in-cheek effort to preserve his memory. Nevertheless, while Fillmore may not have been a great President, he successfully worked to preserve the Union in a peaceful manner when centrifugal tendencies were pulling the sections apart.

Fillmore was born in upstate New York, and became a schoolteacher before studying law. He was admitted to the bar in 1823 and practiced in Buffalo. Harboring a deep-seated suspicion of foreigners and such secret societies as the Masons, he became a political protégé of Thurlow Weed, who was later to become a powerful Whig leader in the state. With his aid, Fillmore was elected to the State Assembly. He later served two terms in Congress, where he joined the Whig Party. In 1844, he was named the Whig candidate for Governor, but lost the election. Fillmore's position against the spread of slavery into the territories was well known, and Henry Clay considered him a good vice presidential candidate to balance the southern, and presumably pro-slavery, standard-bearer, Zachary Taylor, for the Whig ticket in 1848.

Despite his antislavery views, as Vice President, Fillmore presided with fairness over the acrimonious Senate debates about Clay's Compromise of 1850, which were in progress when President Taylor died. As President, Fillmore's moderation in the face of his public views immediately made the passage of the Compromise possible. The bundle of individual bills which he signed admitted California as a free state; organized the New Mexico and Utah Territories, each of which could be admitted to the Union as a free or slave state as its constitution prescribed; gave compensation to Texas for the loss of some territory; abolished the slave trade in the nation's capital; and enacted harsher provisions to recapture fugitive slaves.

Fillmore's presidency is also noted for two other events. First, when Louis Kossuth, the leader of the abortive Hungarian revolt of 1848, visited the United States from 1851 to 1852 in search of aid, the President put a warship at his disposal. Although thousands of Americans cheered the hero, Fillmore made it clear that the United States would not go to war to secure Hungarian independence. Second, in 1852, the President dispatched Commodore Matthew C. Perry to the self-isolated Japanese Empire to open commercial relations. The display of steam powered naval ships in Tokyo Bay so overawed the Japanese that they agreed to establish diplomatic relations with the United States.

Despite his accomplishments, the President's moderation on the slavery issue ultimately pleased neither side, and he was denied renomination. With the demise of the Whigs in 1856, he ran again, this time as the candidate of the American, or Know Nothing, Party, and lost. It was Fillmore's last attempt, and he retired to the presidency of the Buffalo and Erie County Historical Society, a post he kept for the rest of his life. Yet, one memorial to him does survive. The town of Fillmore is the seat of Millard County, Utah.

FRANKLIN PIERCE

November 23, 1804   *October 8, 1869*

President: March 4, 1853 - March 4, 1857

The election of Franklin Pierce is an example of raising the mediocre to the highest office in the land. Although not without talent and experience, this personable, well intentioned, handsome young man was far inferior in intellectual and political ability to the leaders of his Democratic Party. It was only the inability of any of them to capture the nomination that led the convention to name Pierce as its standard-bearer. Yet, the Democrats felt that Pierce had a background good enough for the presidency.

Pierce was born in New Hampshire. His father was a Revolutionary War veteran and served as the state's Governor in 1827 and 1829. Young Pierce graduated from Bowdoin College in 1824 and immediately turned to the practice of law. Like his father, he became a Jacksonian Democrat. As such, he served in the House of Representatives from 1833 to 1837, after which, he became a Senator. Although he then retired to Concord, New Hampshire, where he established a lucrative law practice, he retained his interest in national politics, so much so that President Polk offered him the post of Attorney General in 1846, which he declined.

Pierce was a strong advocate of American territorial expansion. He not only supported the Mexican War, but served in the conflict, rising to the rank of Brigadier General. Although he was a northerner, he detested the abolitionists and supported vigorously the Compromise of 1850. This combination of beliefs made him an acceptable candidate. The country's mood demanded rest from sectional strife, and most people viewed support of the Compromise as likely to assure that result. Consequently, Pierce won election by a decisive margin.

Pierce tried to balance his Cabinet with those of moderate views from all sections, but the rabidly pro-slavery Jefferson Davis, as Secretary of War, became his dominant advisor. In part because of his pro-expansionist views, the President tacitly supported filibustering efforts by private parties invading Cuba and Nicaragua. He also advocated the ratification of the treaty securing the Gadsden Purchase in 1854, which added land from Mexico to the New Mexico Territory to provide a convenient southern railroad route from New Orleans to California.

The President's constant conciliation of the South, however, dismayed northerners. The final break came with his support of the Kansas-Nebraska Bill. Introduced by Senator Stephen A. Douglas of Illinois to ease the tensions over slavery by taking the initiative out of the hands of the Federal government, the bill provided for the creation of the Kansas and Nebraska Territories, whose inhabitants were to decide whether to establish slavery or not. Following a divisive debate in both Congress and the public press, Pierce signed the bill into law. Subsequently, opposing gangs of immigrants sought and shot down each other in "Bleeding Kansas." The violence inflamed public opinion and lost Pierce any chance at renomination. A compromise candidate promising to promote conciliation between the sections thus ended his presidency with a more divided country than when he began it. Pierce spent the rest of his life at Concord, New Hampshire, as an ordinary practicing lawyer.

JAMES BUCHANAN

April 23, 1791   *June 1, 1868*

President: March 4, 1857 - March 4, 1861

When James Buchanan became President, he was almost 66-years old with decades of experience behind him. He was known to be a hard worker, with a great deal of ability. He also possessed tact, a trait important in the conduct of foreign affairs, a task that had consumed most of his public life. In the critical situation which faced the nation, however, strong leadership was needed. Instead, the country got a man whose life consisted of trying to reconcile differences through diplomacy without imposing his own views.

Born the son of a Pennsylvania farmer, by dint of hard work, Buchanan graduated from Dickinson College in 1809, studied law as an apprentice, and became a successful attorney. The sudden death of his fiancee following a lovers' quarrel made him resolve never to marry. Buchanan was thus the first bachelor to enter the White House. He became cautious, peace loving, and soft-spoken.

Originally a Federalist, Buchanan ultimately became a Jacksonian Democrat. He served in Congress from 1821 to 1831 until President Jackson named him Minister to Russia. He returned to serve in the Senate from 1835 to 1845; in the latter year, President Polk named him Secretary of State. As such, he successfully negotiated the Oregon Territory's boundary with Britain. He was also alternatively firm and conciliatory with Mexico until the outbreak of war, a stand which alienated neither North nor South. Because President Pierce appointed him Minister to Britain, Buchanan was outside the country when the issue of slavery was being heatedly debated throughout the country.

Like 1852, the Democratic Convention in 1856 could not agree upon which of its leaders should be its candidate. Buchanan was a northerner who had obtained southern good will by signing the Ostend Manifesto in 1854, along with American Ministers to Spain and France, declaring that the United States was justified in taking Cuba if Spain did not sell it. Buchanan thus became a compromise choice, and, facing no strong opposition after the dissolution of the Whig Party, easily won the election.

Buchanan was a man with a legalistic frame of mind. Moreover, he always liked the company of southerners when he had served in Congress. He abhorred the idea of secession, but he also feared the new Republican Party and the prospect of slave rebellion. Thus, in 1857, he was easily persuaded by southerners in his Cabinet to support the pro-slavery constitution for a projected state of Kansas framed by a rump meeting in the town of Lecompton. The public uproar in the North over this action was reflected in the resulting Congressional debates. Although the Lecompton Constitution was rejected by Congress, Buchanan tried to punish its northern Democratic opponents. This action lost him support in the North, but did not end the danger of secession.

After the Republican victory in 1860 and the secession of the southern states, the President tried diplomacy to reach a settlement. Neither side accepted any compromise. Although Buchanan did turn over a divided nation to his successor, he never legally recognized secession, and he kept Federal troops in military fortifications in the South.

ABRAHAM LINCOLN

February 12, 1809   *April 15, 1865*

President: March 4, 1861 - April 15, 1865

Abraham Lincoln was rejected, reviled, and ridiculed by the majority of the electorate during most of his political life, but during the Civil War, he displayed talents most never suspected he possessed. After his death, the people elevated him to the nation's pantheon to rank with George Washington himself.

Lincoln, born in Kentucky and raised in Indiana and Illinois, reached maturity believing in the Whig program of Federal internal improvements. Following an election loss for the State Legislature as a Whig in 1832, he fought in the Black Hawk War and worked at odd jobs while educating himself by widespread reading and as an apprentice law student. After 1834, he won election to the Legislature for four consecutive terms. Admitted to the bar in 1836, he argued cases succinctly, using humor as a tool. In 1842, he wooed and married Mary Todd, a Kentucky belle, who had stated that she would marry no one but a future President.

Lincoln was elected to Congress, serving from 1847 to 1849, but his courageous opposition to the popular Mexican War denied him reelection. He returned to the law, gaining a reputation for winning cases. The divisive issue of slavery brought him back into politics as an unsuccessful Whig candidate for Senator in 1855. With the dissolution of the Whigs, Lincoln joined the new Republican Party, and, although inexperienced, was named its senatorial candidate in 1858 against the nationally known Democrat, Stephen Douglas. Their debates over slavery earned Lincoln a national reputation despite his loss. He built upon that reputation through a series of public speeches in the following two years. Lincoln was thus well known, although not considered a leader in the new party.

To those who knew him, however, it was clear that this tall, lanky, misshapen man, with his melancholy expression and fund of amusing tales was really a shrewd and astute politician. He had courage and a sense of timing. He knew when to be patient and when to act. He could take the measure of a man, and using a combination of wit, charm, argument, and political maneuver, make him do what he wished. Lincoln was a leader when the nation surely needed one.

At the 1860 Republican Convention, the submission of Lincoln's name provoked the first spontaneous demonstration in history. The enthusiasm helped sway Republican leaders to nominate him as their candidate. The disruption of the Democratic Party over slavery insured his election. Some southern states, knowing Lincoln's antislavery views, then seceded. Throughout the Civil War, Lincoln's aim was the preservation of the Union, and he exercised unparalleled executive power to attain it, including issuing the Emancipation Proclamation. Although criticized in his lifetime, Lincoln's assassination by John Wilkes Booth, an actor and southern sympathizer, on Good Friday following the successful conclusion of the war, changed people's views of the President. To them, if George Washington was the Father of the Country, then Lincoln was the Savior who suffered and died for the cause.

ANDREW JOHNSON

December 29, 1808   *July 31, 1875*

President: April 15, 1865 - March 4, 1869

Andrew Johnson's life is an example of the American ideal of the poor boy who, by dint of hard work, becomes President of the United States. Unfortunately, political circumstances did not make his presidency a successful one.

Johnson was born the son of a porter at an inn in North Carolina, and, at the age of fourteen, was apprenticed to a tailor. In 1826, he settled in eastern Tennessee, where he opened a small shop and married Eliza McCaudle a year later. Because he had little schooling, Johnson's bride undertook to teach the tailor how to write, and by 1828, he was elected Mayor of his town of Greenville. He became known for his debating ability and his unwavering support of the interest of the small farmers and craftsmen of his region against that of the large slaveholders who dominated western Tennessee. Because of this, he was elected to the State Legislature and then to Congress, where he served from 1846 to 1855. In Congress, this young Democrat in 1846 introduced the first Homestead Bill to permit farmers to settle on western lands.

Johnson accepted the institution of slavery, and even owned some slaves in his lifetime. Although he disliked abolitionists, he felt that slavery should not be extended to the territories. With these views, he was elected Governor of Tennessee for two successful terms, and then to the Senate, where he took his seat in 1857. When the Democratic Party fell apart in 1860, he supported presidential candidate John Crittenden of Kentucky, a man in favor of preserving the Union and whose views on slavery were similar to his own.

When Tennessee seceded in June, 1861, Johnson remained loyal to the Union and stayed in his Senate seat. This southern Democrat thus achieved national attention. His vigorous support of Lincoln's policies led the President to appoint him military Governor of Tennessee in 1862 after the Federal army had obtained control of sufficient territory there. Johnson performed with skill his thankless task of restoring civil government. His success convinced him that the rights of the states could continue to be recognized. It also made him a candidate for Vice President with Lincoln on the 1864 Union Party ticket, a combination of Republicans and War Democrats created to appeal to as wide a constituency as possible.

Lincoln's assassination in 1865 thrust Johnson into the presidency. Strong, patriotic, industrious, and honest, Johnson tried to carry out Lincoln's practical and compassionate plans for the restoration of the southern states into the Union. Unfortunately, Johnson was politically isolated as a Democrat in a Republican-dominated administration with an increasingly Radical Republican Congress that wished to punish the South. When opposed, Johnson became pugnacious and stubborn. The conflict between the President and Congress culminated near the end of his term in Johnson's impeachment by the House of Representatives; the Senate failed to convict by only one vote. The major triumph of his administration, the purchase of Alaska, was ridiculed at the time and not appreciated until decades later. After his presidency, Johnson returned to private life. He was finally vindicated, however, when returned to the Senate in 1875.

ULYSSES SIMPSON GRANT

April 27, 1822   *July 23, 1885*

President: March 4, 1869 - March 4, 1877

Hiram Ulysses Grant would have been the name of a President if it had not been for an error by a West Point clerk. This son of an Ohio farmer, upon arrival at the military academy, discovered that he was entered on the roles as Ulysses Simpson Grant, and he decided to keep the new name. Grant thus became the first President to have his name changed.

Upon graduation in 1843, Grant was commissioned a Second Lieutenant and served in the Mexican War under both Generals Zachary Taylor and Winfield Scott. His men liked his simple, modest, and honest character. Following the war, he was posted to the West but an accusation of excessive drinking led him to resign his commission in 1854. Grant, a trained and tested military man who had no other skills, except, perhaps, his love and care of horses, floundered in civilian life. He tried farming and real estate, but ended as a clerk in his father's leather store in southern Illinois. Those who knew him deemed him a failure.

Politics had not been a major concern in Grant's life. He was not an abolitionist, but he did not defend slavery either, and the only vote he had cast for President was for the Democrat, James Buchanan, in 1856. With the outbreak of the Civil War, he gave his total loyalty to the Union.

The Governor of Illinois appointed Grant a Colonel at the outbreak of the war, but President Lincoln, upon the recommendation of Grant's Congressman, shortly raised him to the rank of Brigadier General. A series of victories, notably one at Vicksburg, brought the cigar-smoking, stoop-shouldered, bearded general with his simple, unkempt uniform to Lincoln's attention. His demand that his opponents agree to unconditional surrender also brought him popular acclaim as General "Unconditional Surrender" Grant. In March, 1864, Lincoln appointed him to the newly revived rank of Lieutenant General with command of the entire Union army. His relentless pursuit of Confederate troops and his constant attack, despite its cost in human lives, resulted in Union victory. Grant was not a vindictive person, and offered General Robert E. Lee moderate surrender terms.

The Civil War made Grant a popular hero and a presidential prospect. In 1866, he was raised to a full General, and, in 1867, President Johnson named him interim Secretary of War. By walking a fine line between the President and Congress, Grant retained his prospects. He was nominated by the Republican Convention, and with a fund of good will in both North and South, won election after a bitter campaign. The great general, however, was unfit to handle political and governmental problems. Simple and honest, he was naive about his appointees and advisors, and unaware of their widespread corruption. An unsuccessful businessman, he admired those who made fortunes, including the unscrupulous robber barons of the age, and accepted such gifts as fine horses from them as his due. Grant provided no leadership, letting Congress do its will. Yet, even after the scandals of his administration became public and his term of office ceased, he remained a popular hero. In his final days, penniless and suffering from throat cancer, he rushed to successfully complete his wartime memoirs to leave his wife and children with adequate financial resources.

RUTHERFORD BIRCHARD HAYES

October 4, 1822   *January 17, 1893*

President: March 4, 1877 - March 4, 1881

Rutherford B. Hayes was born the posthumous son of an Ohio farmer and was raised by his uncle. He graduated from Kenyon College in 1843 and then from Harvard Law School, after which he set up legal practice in Cincinnati, serving as that city's Solicitor from 1858 to 1861. With the outbreak of the Civil War, he volunteered for service as a Major despite the fact that, by that time, he had a wife and family. He compiled a record for bravery, and was wounded at the Battle of Antietam. At war's end, he was a Major General.

Utilizing his war record, Hayes was elected to Congress, serving from 1865 to 1867. He later served as Governor of Ohio, 1867 to 1871. He then ran for Congress again, but lost, only to be reelected for another two-year gubernatorial term in 1874. In office, he gained a reputation as an honest man with moderate views. On one of the important issues of the day, whether to increase the amount of money in circulation to inflate the currency, he campaigned for sound money. This brought him national attention and won him the Republican presidential nomination in 1876.

The election was marked by controversy. Both Hayes and the Democrat, Samuel J. Tilden, claimed victory, but the issue was clouded when Oregon, Florida, Louisiana, and South Carolina each submitted two returns, each indicating a different candidate as the winner. In the absence of Constitutional guidelines, Congress appointed an Electoral Commission of eight Republicans and seven Democrats made up of members of the House of Representatives, the Senate, and the Supreme Court. By a partisan vote of eight to seven in each case, the Republican returns were declared valid. Although Tilden had won the popular vote, Hayes emerged with a one vote Electoral College majority and was declared President.

As President, Hayes withdrew Federal troops from the South, thus ending Reconstruction. He appointed a strong Cabinet which did much to clean up the corruption of the Grant era. This placed Hayes in opposition to many party leaders who regarded Federal offices chiefly as positions for those who were loyal mainly to themselves, regardless of fitness for the job. Hayes even forbade Federal workers to take part in political activities. On the money issue, he vetoed bills to expand the currency in circulation by coining silver, and demanded all payments be made in gold. His solution to the outbreak of an unprecedented railroad strike in 1877 was to send Federal troops to break it.

Hayes was a genial man, but he was also stubborn and inwardly nervous. In politics, he tried to be temperate and cautious, but he hated to make controversial decisions. He thus felt that Congress should take the lead in solving the nation's problems. As President, he totally abstained from the consumption of alcohol, and even refused to serve wine at state dinners, although the White House steward surreptitiously provided foreign diplomats with a spiked "Roman Punch" at luncheons. His controversial election seemed to taint his legitimacy in office. This, combined with his quarrel with Republican leaders on the patronage question, made him unpopular, and he knew it. Tired of his high office, he refused to run for a second term.

JAMES ABRAM GARFIELD

November 19, 1831   *September 19, 1881*

President: March 4, 1881 - September 19, 1881

James A. Garfield was one of the few Presidents to have been born in a real log cabin. He grew up in poverty on his Ohio farm. Life became more difficult at the age of two when his father died. As a youngster, in addition to farming, Garfield earned money as a canal bargeman and a carpenter. For his education, he attended Western Reserve Eclectic, later Hiram College, and was graduated from Williams College in 1856. He returned to Hiram to teach Greek and Latin in 1857, and later became Principal. He also studied law and was admitted to the bar in 1859. That year, he also served in the Ohio Senate.

At the outbreak of the Civil War in 1861, Garfield resigned his seat to organize a volunteer regiment. Starting as a Lieutenant

Colonel, Garfield saw action in several battles in the western the-atre of the war, showing himself an excellent battlefield comman-der and a good disciplinarian. In two years, he rose to the rank of Major General and chief of staff to General William Rosecrans.

In 1863, Garfield resigned his commission to run for election to the House of Representatives. He won and took the seat, which he held continually until 1880. A studious man and a good orator, he won the respect of his colleagues in the House because of his industriousness and constant adherence to the Republican Party's program. He went along with the policy of Congress on Reconstruction, sound money, and party patronage. Although he believed in low tariffs for imports, he fiercely defended the high tariff interests of the manufacturers of his district. If Garfield had one drawback, it was his indecisiveness. He wanted to be liked and to do the right thing, and he thus often vacillated.

The Republican Convention in 1880 was deeply divided. Grant hoped for a third term; "Stalwarts," like Roscoe Conkling, who wanted to use the civil service for pure party patronage, backed John Sherman; while the "Half-Breeds," who wished to be more circumspect about patronage, upheld the candidacy of James G. Blaine. When, after 35 ballots, no one had won the nomination, the convention turned to the nationally unknown Garfield, who received the unexpected candidacy on the 36th ballot. Garfield was able to win the subsequent election by a narrow margin.

Once in office, the vacillating Garfield stood in the middle of his party's battle over patronage. His appointment of Blaine as Secretary of State caused Senator Conkling and the "Stalwarts" to oppose the President vigorously at every turn, and they were out-raged when Garfield called for an investigation of abuses in the Post Office and appointed a "Half-Breed" as the Collector of the Port of New York. Yet, Garfield agonized over every appointment he had to make, a process that made him miserable.

It was the patronage issue that finally killed him. On July 2, 1881, Garfield was shot in a Washington railroad station by Charles Guiteau, a lawyer who was a disappointed "Stalwart" office seeker. Mortally wounded, the President clung to life through the sweltering summer, finally succumbing two months later, after serving only six months as the nation's chief executive.

CHESTER ALAN ARTHUR

October 5, 1829   *November 18, 1886*

President: September 19, 1881 - March 4, 1885

Chester A. Arthur is an example of a man who grew in the job. Considered a party hack when he entered the presidency, his conduct in office proved quite statesmanlike.

Born in Vermont to a Scots-Irish clergyman, Arthur was educated at Union College, from which he graduated in 1848. He then taught school in Vermont, but seeking greater opportunity, he moved to New York City, studied law, and established his legal practice there. On the question of slavery, he was an abolitionist, became an early member of the new Republican Party, and played a very active role in local party affairs.

Arthur became so prominent among New York City Republicans for his unstinting work on their behalf, that, on the recommendation of New York's Senator Roscoe Conkling, President Grant appointed him Collector of the Port of New York in 1871. Because the port was the nation's largest, the Collector commanded an army of appointees, who Arthur made sure were all fellow Republicans rewarded for their party loyalty. This included the author, Herman Melville, who was named an outdoor inspector. Arthur was personally honest in his conduct of the office, and a good administrator. He would not stay out of party politics, however, and, for this, he was removed in 1878 by President Hayes, who had forbidden such activity. Nevertheless, in 1880, Arthur, as Conkling's henchman, was nominated for Vice President by the Republicans to satisfy the "Stalwarts" after Garfield was named the compromise presidential candidate.

The only elective office Arthur ever held was Vice President. Six months after assuming that office, he became chief executive when President Garfield succumbed to an assassin's bullet. Much to the astonishment of many who desired to reform the civil service, but despaired that a political hack now was President, Arthur became a transformed man. Garfield had been a victim of the system of partisan appointments, and the new President cut his ties with the "Stalwarts" to raise himself above politics. He continued Garfield's investigation of the Post Office, and vigorously supported the movement for civil service reform. He signed into law an act creating the Civil Service Commission to administer competitive examinations for about ten percent of all government jobs. The same law made it illegal to force officeholders to make political contributions. As President, Arthur got Congress to create a nonpartisan tariff commission to suggest reductions, and he urged Congress to adopt its recommendations. He also became the first to come out for railroad regulation to end abuses.

Arthur was a genial man who liked good food and flashy clothes. He was also a systematic, thoughtful, businesslike, and considerate administrator who worked hard to restore dignity to the presidency. Politically, however, he was a failure. The "Stalwarts" detested him for deserting their cause, and the "Half-Breeds" could not forget his "Stalwart" past. He was thus denied the Republican nomination he sought in 1884.

GROVER CLEVELAND

March 18, 1837   *June 24, 1908*

President: March 4, 1885 - March 4, 1889; March 4, 1893 - March 4, 1897

Grover Cleveland was the first President to be elected to two nonconsecutive terms, to be nominated by his party for three terms consecutively, and to be married in the White House. He was also the first to leave the country during his presidency when his cancerous lower jaw was replaced with a hard rubber one during a secret operation on a naval ship outside the territorial limits.

Born in New Jersey, Cleveland was baptized with the first name, Stephen, which he dropped upon reaching maturity. His father, a Presbyterian minister, moved the family to upstate New York, and died when Cleveland was fifteen years old. Young

Grover started working as a clerk, taught at a school for the blind, then apprenticed himself to a law office, and was admitted to the bar in 1859. He avoided the Civil War draft by paying for a substitute to take his place in the ranks, a tactic permitted by law. Instead, he became an Assistant District Attorney in Erie County in 1863 and Sheriff in 1871.

Cleveland's rise to the presidency was meteoric. Although he lacked social grace, he had integrity, and was chosen by reformers as a candidate for Mayor of Buffalo to throw out a corrupt political machine. In 1881, as Mayor, he gained such a reputation for honesty that he was elected Governor of New York as a Democrat the following year. There, his opposition to New York City's corrupt Tammany Hall brought him the Democratic presidential nomination in 1884. During the campaign, his public admission of fathering an illegitimate child was offered as proof of his honesty, and he won election by a narrow margin.

In his first term, Cleveland emphasized civil service reform, sound money, and moderate tariffs. He insisted upon honesty and efficiency in administration. A stubborn man, he could sometimes be inflexible. Renominated in 1888, he won a majority of the popular vote, but his opponent won narrowly in enough populous states to win the vote in the Electoral College. Un-daunted, his wife, Frances, promised the White House servants that they would return four years later, and they did.

During Cleveland's second term, however, conditions were different. The Panic of 1893 brought on a severe economic depression. Always a sound money man, the President opposed any attempt at inflating the currency by coining silver, and, as an opponent of excessive spending, he vetoed Federal aid to suffering farmers. He also sent Federal troops to break a strike at the Pullman Company in 1894. Cleveland thus alienated farmers, silver miners, and laborers. His chief success came in foreign affairs when he backed his Secretary of State, Richard Olney, whose assertion that the United States was sovereign in the Western Hemisphere was used in an effort to get Britain to arbitrate a boundary dispute between British Guiana and Venezuela. The Democrats, nevertheless, repudiated Cleveland's domestic policies at their 1896 Convention, but he continued to remain a symbol of honesty and integrity for years after his retirement.

BENJAMIN HARRISON

August 20, 1833   *March 13, 1901*

President: March 4, 1889 - March 4, 1893

Like John Quincy Adams, Benjamin Harrison was born to a presidential tradition; his grandfather, William Henry Harrison, had been a President before him. His great grandfather, after whom he was named, had signed the Declaration of Independence. His father, John Scott Harrison, had served in Congress. Even so, his chief claim to fame is that he was the first President to be succeeded by his predecessor.

Born in Indiana, Harrison was first educated on his father's farm. His outstanding intelligence, however, brought him to Miami University from where he graduated in 1852 at the age of eighteen. He was admitted to the bar the following year, and established a lucrative practice as a corporation lawyer in Indianapolis. He also spent a number of years as a State Supreme Court reporter. Harrison joined the army during the Civil War, fought under General William Sherman, and was discharged with the brevet rank of Brigadier General.

Harrison's political career began in 1876 when the Republicans nominated him for Governor of Indiana, although he lost the election. He was more successful when he ran for the Senate. During his term from 1881 to 1887, he served as a faithful Republican. Most notably, he worked for pensions for the veterans of the Civil War, a measure President Cleveland vetoed as too expensive.

At the Republican Convention in 1888, party leaders were sharply divided among a number of possible candidates. Harrison's name was offered as a way out of the deadlock, especially when a former Senate colleague vouched for his support of a protective tariff. In the election, President Cleveland won a small majority of the total popular vote, but Harrison had narrowly captured the votes of enough industrial states to give him the majority in the Electoral College and to make him President.

As President, Harrison was dignified, honest, and able, but, as a man of keen intelligence, he did not suffer fools gladly. He came across as having a cold personality. He gave lip service to civil service reform, appointing Theodore Roosevelt as Civil Service Commissioner, but he did nothing to support the idea. His Secretary of State, James G. Blaine, controlled appointments. He let Congress, under the tight control of Speaker of the House Thomas B. Reed, take the leadership in setting policy, and he signed into law a high tariff, the Sherman Antitrust Act, and the Sherman Silver Purchase Act. When Civil War veterans' pensions were augmented by Congress, unlike President Cleveland, he supported the measure.

Although hardly popular, even among the political leaders who selected him four years earlier, Harrison bestirred himself to secure renomination at the Republican Convention of 1892. In the election, however, he suffered a resounding defeat at the hands of Cleveland. Harrison, who lost even in his own state of Indiana, returned home to resume his law practice.

WILLIAM MCKINLEY

January 29, 1843   *September 14, 1901*

President: March 4, 1897 - September 14, 1901

William McKinley's presidency marked a watershed. It retained the policies of the immediate past in domestic affairs; but in foreign affairs, it looked forward to the future.

Born the son of an Ohio ironmaker, McKinley attended Allegheny College before enlisting as a private at the age of eighteen to fight in the Civil War in the same Ohio unit as Major Rutherford B. Hayes. He eventually became a Captain, and, in 1865, he received the brevet rank of Major. He then studied at the law school in Albany, New York, before returning to Ohio to establish his practice. He became active in Republican politics, campaigning vigorously for the election of General Grant. He won his own election to the House of Representatives in 1876, and retained his seat, except for the 1883 - 1885 term, until 1891.

Handsome, devout, and kindly, McKinley emerged as a defender of industrialists. He believed this stance would enhance his own position in Ohio politics and that of his party. He thus supported laws allowing the Federal government to buy silver to help western silver miners, and consistently supported a high tariff to protect American industry. He was even the architect of the protectionist McKinley Tariff of 1890.

His policies induced Ohio industrialist and political leader, Mark Hanna, to guide McKinley's career. Hanna got him elected Governor of Ohio, where he served from 1892 to 1896, and secured him the 1896 Republican presidential nomination. The big issue of the day was the free coinage of silver, which would lead to inflation. Under Hanna's direction, McKinley stood firmly for the gold standard and campaigned from his own front porch, rather than compete with his opponent, the great orator William Jennings Bryan, on the stump. McKinley won by a decisive margin.

Since the President knew Congress and its ways, he got on well with it, and was conciliatory. The discovery of Alaskan gold increased the currency in circulation and eased the depression without resorting to methods opposed by big business. In following the lead of Congress in domestic affairs, the President aped his immediate predecessors. In foreign policy, however, McKinley was unexpectedly drawn into the Spanish-American War over Cuba by lurid press coverage of events and the sinking of the *Maine* in Havana harbor. As a result of the war, the President demanded the Philippines from Spain and tight American control of Cuba. In addition, Puerto Rico was annexed. In a separate action, McKinley recommended that American sovereignty be extended to Hawaii. Also, McKinley tried to stake out a place for the country in the China trade by supporting the idea of the Open Door. For the first time, the United States obtained an overseas colonial empire, a circumstance which caused much public debate over whether it was compatible with American ideals of liberty. This might have led Leon Czolgosz, an anarchist, to shoot the President as he was shaking hands with citizens at the Pan-American Exposition in Buffalo on September 6, 1901. McKinley died eight days later, and for the first time, a presidential funeral was filmed by a motion picture cameraman.

THEODORE ROOSEVELT

October 27, 1858   *January 6, 1919*

President: September 14, 1901 - March 4, 1909

Few expected Theodore Roosevelt, scion of an old New York colonial family, son of a prosperous glass importer, and graduate of Harvard, who was saddled with a high, squeaky voice and a body enfeebled by youthful asthma to become a national embodiment of vigor and dynamism and the popular idol of hardworking shopkeepers and laborers. Through determination and hard work, he overcame his illness, and a two-year sojourn working on a Dakota Territory cattle ranch produced a love of the great outdoors and a lifelong friendship with western cowboys.

Roosevelt was shocked at the low ethical standards of industrialists and the governmental corruption they produced in his day. He wanted reform, but realized that he could do nothing unless he were in office, and that meant he had to play politics by accommodating party leaders. He joined the Republican Party, and served in the New York Assembly from 1881 to 1884. As he rose in party esteem, he was appointed to the United States Civil Service Commission, then President of the New York City Board of Police Commissioners, and then Assistant Secretary of the Navy. In the latter role, he dispatched Admiral George Dewey's fleet to Manila before the outbreak of the Spanish-American War to put it in position to take the Philippines once hostilities began. He resigned in 1898 to organize his volunteer Rough Riders, with whom he won fame in the Battle of San Juan Hill.

His popularity made him Governor of New York in 1899, but his zealous actions against corruption induced party leaders to nominate him for Vice President under McKinley in 1900 to get rid of him. The President's assassination, however, made Roosevelt the nation's chief executive.

As President, Roosevelt opposed monopolies not operating in the national interest and demanded a "square deal" for labor. He advocated railroad and bank regulation, civil service reform, and a widespread conservation program. Overseas, he encouraged a revolution in Panama that led to the building of the Panama Canal, brought an end to the Russo-Japanese War, an action which won him the Nobel Peace Prize, and sent American delegates to the Algeciras Conference on the question of Morocco. At the end of his presidency, he practically dictated the nomination of his successor, William Howard Taft.

Nevertheless, Roosevelt had become disenchanted with Taft by 1912. Denied nomination by the Republicans that year, his supporters formed the new Progressive Party for him to run again. His remark that he felt like a bull moose caused reporters to call it the Bull Moose Party. Although Roosevelt came in second, a remarkable feat for a third party candidacy, this was his last political campaign.

Roosevelt, the youngest man to become President, caught the imagination of the electorate with more than his policies. His refusal to shoot a bear cub on a hunting trip led to the creation of the toy "Teddy" bear named for him, and his remark that an inn's coffee was "good to the last drop" became a successful slogan for selling it throughout the country. Perhaps his most lasting legacy, however, is the huge acreage he added to national parks and national forests, thus focussing attention on the preservation of the environment.

WILLIAM HOWARD TAFT

September 15, 1857   *March 8, 1930*

President: March 4, 1909 - March 4, 1913

William Howard Taft carried more than the burdens of the presidency when he entered the White House. He weighed about 300 pounds, and an oversized bathtub had to be installed in the mansion for him. His weight may have accounted for his inclination to neglect the political dimensions of his office. This disposition may also have been caused by his judicial temperament, however.

Taft was born into a politically prominent Ohio family. His father, Alonzo Taft, served under President Grant as Secretary of War and then as Attorney General; President Arthur named him Minister to Austria and then to Russia. Young William, meanwhile, graduated from Yale in 1878, and from Cincinnati Law School in 1880. He first reported law for Cincinnati newspapers, then served as Assistant Prosecuting Attorney from 1881 to 1883, Assistant County Solicitor in 1885, and Judge of the Superior Court in 1887. President Benjamin Harrison gave young Taft national attention when he appointed him Solicitor General, where he served from 1890 to 1892. In 1892, Taft was appointed Federal Circuit Judge.

In 1900, President McKinley tapped Taft to head a commission to provide civil government for the Philippines, a task which was completed in eighteen months. His success secured him appointment as the first civil Governor of the islands, where he spent the happiest years of his life, from 1901 to 1904.

President Roosevelt called Taft home to serve as Secretary of War, his father's old post, from 1904 to 1908. Informally, he was the President's troubleshooter, and a grateful Roosevelt persuaded him to accept the Republican nomination for the presidency. With Roosevelt's backing, he won election handily.

Taft wanted to continue his predecessor's reform program, and he succeeded to a remarkable degree. Postal savings banks and parcel post were established, a corporate income tax was begun, and more monopolies were taken to court for violating the laws than under Roosevelt. Unfortunately, Taft was more of a constitutional lawyer than a politician. He did not want to antagonize the Republican leaders of Congress. He signed a high protective tariff into law and fired Gifford Pinchot, a staunch conservationist and friend of Roosevelt, as the head of the Forestry Service. These actions antagonized those Republicans who had supported Roosevelt, and they urged the former President to run again. A rift developed between the two friends which was never repaired. Taft received the Republican nomination for reelection in 1912, but the defection of Roosevelt and his supporters doomed his candidacy.

Taft then taught law at Yale from 1913 to 1921, taking some time during World War I to act as co-chairman of the National War Labor Board from 1918 to 1919. In 1921, he was appointed by President Warren G. Harding to the post he had always desired, Chief Justice of the United States. Taft thus became the first President to subsequently serve on the Supreme Court.

WOODROW WILSON

December 28, 1856   *February 3, 1924*

President: March 4, 1913 - March 4, 1921

Thomas Woodrow Wilson, was born in Virginia, the son of a strict Presbyterian minister. Wilson was raised in Georgia and in the Carolinas during the Reconstruction era. Both circumstances marked his character. The second made him a lifelong Democrat opposed to economic oppression; the first made him a moral and idealistic adult opposed to compromise once he determined that he was right. As an adult, he also ceased using his first name.

After attending Davidson College, Wilson received his B.A. from Princeton in 1879, then studied law at the University of Virginia before practicing in Atlanta in 1882. Disenchanted with the law, he obtained his Ph.D. in government and history at Johns Hopkins in 1886. Entering academic life, he taught at Bryn Mawr and

Wesleyan before becoming Professor of Jurisprudence and Political Science at Princeton in 1890. A stimulating teacher, he was chosen the university's President in 1902, the first not a member of the ministry. He was an effective leader in instituting educational reforms, but was unable to compromise with an increasingly strong opposition. By 1910, he felt he had to resign.

The favorable publicity generated by his academic reforms encouraged New Jersey Democratic political leaders to nominate him for Governor. They mistakenly thought they could control him, but Wilson brought the same reforming zeal to his new post. This gained him national attention and the Democratic Convention's nomination in 1912. The split in Republican ranks between Taft and Roosevelt supporters that year won him the presidency.

As President, Wilson imitated a British Prime Minister, working closely with his party's members in Congress, rewarding those who acted with him and punishing those who opposed him. Knowing he could sway people to act for the loftiest ideals through his eloquence, he revived the practice, dormant since Jefferson, of speaking to Congress in person. He also was the first President to hold regular press conferences. He was thus able to obtain lower tariff rates, to establish the Federal Reserve System and the Federal Trade Commission, to ease credit for farmers, and to obtain an eight-hour day for railroad workers. In foreign affairs, he took a moral stance, especially in dealing with aspects of the Mexican Revolution. He vainly tried to mediate between the two sides on the outbreak of World War I in Europe. His successful reelection bid in 1916 was fought on the slogan, "He kept us out of war," although the President himself did not approve it. Germany's resumption of unrestricted submarine warfare caused Wilson to ask Congress to declare war in 1917, and to propose the Fourteen Points in 1918 as a basis for the peace settlement.

In 1919, Wilson became the first President to head a peace delegation and to attend a summit conference. Viewing his League of Nations embodied in the peace treaty as a moral question, he refused to compromise, and collapsed from a stroke while on a nationwide speaking tour to whip up American support. Partially paralyzed, Wilson ended his presidency as an invalid communicating only with his wife and physician, bitterly disappointed that his vision for a peaceful world had been rejected.

WARREN GAMALIEL HARDING

November 2, 1865   *August 2, 1923*

President: March 4, 1921 - August 2, 1923

Warren G. Harding was born in Ohio, the son of a physician, and attended Ohio Central College from 1879 to 1882. He then studied law briefly before becoming the owner and editor of a small town newspaper. An amiable man, loyal to his friends, Harding loved to spend time around a card table, drinking and smoking. His mind was hardly penetrating, but his statesmanlike face, combined with his unquestioned loyalty, proved attractive to Republican Party leaders. He first served as a State Senator from 1900 to 1904 before becoming Lieutenant Governor for two years. In 1910, he was nominated for Governor, but lost the election.

In 1914, Harding won election to the Senate, and he loved the job. He was a loyal Republican during World War I, voting against Federal control of food and fuel, but for an anti-strike law, women's suffrage, and Prohibition. In 1916, he gained some national attention by serving as Temporary Chairman of the Republican Convention. He prided himself on his speaking ability, although his oratory, while holding the interest of an audience, either beat an old idea to death or served to obscure the absence of ideas by leaving his hearers believing he espoused whatever they supported.

At the 1920 Convention, Harding's friend, Henry Daugherty, predicted correctly that the candidates for nomination would be deadlocked and that party leaders would then meet in a "smoke-filled room" to name Harding as the nominee. The leaders agreed Harding was the least objectionable candidate, and he was duly nominated. In the campaign, Harding campaigned for a "return to normalcy," an innocuous phrase, and straddled the question of joining the League of Nations. In this election, the first in which women were allowed to vote all over the nation, Harding won handily.

Harding knew he was unsuited to the presidency. He simply could not understand some things, such as some aspects of the budget, he was required to know. Wisely, he determined to appoint to office intelligent and experienced people who could do the job. Secretary of State Charles Evans Hughes, Secretary of the Treasury Andrew W. Mellon, and Secretary of Commerce Herbert Hoover were first-class appointments. Harding, however, could not overcome his genial, trusting, and amiable nature, and he appointed some of his card playing cronies as well, including Daugherty as Attorney General, Albert B. Fall as Secretary of the Interior, and Edwin Denby as Secretary of the Navy.

Harding's administration was responsible for the Washington Naval Treaty, the first pact ever to reduce armaments, and for beginning the prosperity of the 1920s. Betrayal by the President's friends, however, resulted in outright bribery, misuse of Veterans' Administration funds, and the giveaway of government oil to private interests. Harding's discovery of these actions caused a rise in his blood pressure and sleepless nights. A speaking trip to Alaska provided no cure, and Harding died suddenly in San Francisco of mysterious causes, but probably of apoplexy. The public, not yet informed of the scandals, wept openly at the death of a popular President.

CALVIN COOLIDGE

July 4, 1872   *January 5, 1933*

President: August 2, 1923 - March 4, 1929

Calvin Coolidge was born in Vermont and baptized with the first name John, but, like Presidents Cleveland and Wilson, he used only his middle name after his childhood. His father was a storekeeper and became a local Justice of the Peace. Young Coolidge left his small farming community to work his way through Amherst College in nearby Massachusetts, graduating in 1895. He stayed in Massachusetts, setting up a law practice in Northampton. Joining the Republican Party, Coolidge rose in local and state politics beginning with election as Mayor of Northampton, followed by service in the State Senate, then election as Lieutenant Governor, and finally as Governor, serving from 1919 to 1920.

Coolidge was Governor when World War I ended and a wave of industrial strikes broke out throughout the country. Many people panicked believing that the recent Bolshevik Revolution in Russia was being exported to the United States. When the Boston police force also struck, Governor Coolidge took quick action by sending the state National Guard to patrol the streets and thus break the strike. His remark, "There is no right to strike against the public safety by anybody, anywhere, anytime," made him a national hero. Consequently, at the 1920 Republican Convention, after the delegates dutifully ratified their leaders' choice of Harding as their presidential candidate, they balked at their selection for Vice President and insisted on nominating Coolidge for that post.

When President Harding suddenly died, Coolidge was awakened by his father at the family home in Vermont and immediately took the oath which his father administered in his capacity as Justice of the Peace. As President, Coolidge dealt with the scandals caused by President Harding's appointees as they became public by dismissing the culprits and by announcing he stood for public honesty. He was not stained by the scandals and easily won election in his own right in 1924.

Coolidge, true to his Yankee heritage, lived frugally, but he admired wealthy men. This, combined with his preference for the Republican policies of the pre-Roosevelt era of his youth without tolerating its corruption, made him favor high tariffs, tax reduction, and government support of industry. He fully believed that the Federal government should do next to nothing, and spent a good portion of every afternoon napping. He used the veto against a veteran's bonus (which Congress overrode) and farm relief bills. The President also had a reputation for taciturnity, and was nicknamed "Silent Cal." He calculated that he would not be hurt by what he did not say. Yet, his was the first voice of a President to be broadcast over radio at an inaugural, and he was the first President to appear in a sound film newsreel.

Coolidge, dour, abstemious, laconic, and unimaginative, was also respectable, parsimonious, and democratic in his habits. Oddly, he was highly popular in an era noted for its extravagance and its revolution in manners and morals against a more prim Victorian past.

HERBERT CLARK HOOVER

August 10, 1874   *October 20, 1964*

President: March 4, 1929 - March 4, 1933

Few Presidents were more admired upon inauguration than Herbert Hoover; and few were more vilified by the American public upon leaving office. Having great administrative gifts and humanitarian impulses, he was forced to face the onset of the disastrous Great Depression with inadequate political skills and a dogged adherence to an unworkable political theory.

Hoover was born in Iowa, the son of a Quaker blacksmith, and grew up in Indian Territory (now Oklahoma) and Oregon. He was graduated from Stanford in 1891 with a B.A. in engineering. After working with the United States Geological Survey and with mines in the West, he went abroad, earning a fortune as a mining engineer in Australia, Asia, Europe, and Africa, as well as in America. While working for the imperial mines in China in 1900, he directed food relief for those affected by the Boxer Rebellion. Having amassed enough money, Hoover decided to devote the rest of his life to public service.

His experience in China proved valuable when he directed the American Relief Committee in London in the early years of World War I and the United States Committee for Relief in Belgium for the remainder of the conflict. From 1917 to 1919, he also acted as President Wilson's Food Administrator, and from 1918 to 1923, he led the American Relief Administration feeding children in the defeated nations. He also organized Russian Relief to feed those starving in the Russian Civil War from 1918 to 1923.

Hoover's reputation as a humanitarian and administrator led to his appointment by President Harding as Secretary of Commerce. The appointment was renewed by President Coolidge. Hoover was a great Commerce Secretary, establishing the standardization of products, encouraging the formation of trade associations among businesses, and finding export markets for American goods. He clearly earned the Republican nomination for the presidency in 1928, and he was elected for the first time to any office.

To combat the Great Depression following the stock market crash of October 1929, the President relied upon private charities and state governments to provide relief for the unemployed. He firmly believed that the Federal government had no right to perform that function. He did authorize the construction of public works, but the number was too few to employ the masses out of work. He exhorted businessmen not to cut wages, but sluggish sales dictated wage reduction and layoffs. He finally agreed to the establishment of the Reconstruction Finance Corporation to lend funds to banks facing bankruptcy, but his lack of political skill made it seem he was ready to aid big business and do nothing to help the average man.

Consequently, Hoover lost reelection decisively, unjustly saddled with causing the Great Depression. It was not until 1947 that an American President, Harry S Truman, called upon his skills to coordinate the European Food Program, and to chair a commission for reorganizing the executive branch. When he died at the age of 90, he was only a few months short of John Adams's longevity record for former Presidents.

FRANKLIN DELANO ROOSEVELT

January 30, 1882   *April 12, 1945*

President: March 4, 1933 - April 12, 1945

Franklin Delano Roosevelt broke more precedents than any other President. He was the first to accept his convention's nomination in person; the first to be inaugurated on January 20th (in 1937); the first to be elected to four terms; the first to appear on television (1939); the first to have a crippling handicap; the first to have a politically active First Lady (Eleanor); and the first to appoint a woman, Frances Perkins, to a Cabinet post. He was the chief executive in the midst of two crises, the Great Depression and World War II, exercising unparalleled leadership and achieving great public popularity.

Roosevelt, born into a patrician family in upstate New York, was a Democrat. After graduating from Harvard in 1904 and attending Columbia Law School, he was admitted to the bar.

Blessed with a famous name because of his distant cousin, Theodore Roosevelt, he successfully ran for the State Senate, where he served from 1910 to 1913, and gained a reputation as an anti-Tammany Democrat. His vigorous campaigning on behalf of Woodrow Wilson brought him appointment as Assistant Secretary of the Navy, the same post his cousin, Theodore, had occupied. His name also helped gain him nomination for the vice presidency in 1920 on the ticket that was defeated by Warren Harding.

In the summer of 1921, Roosevelt was stricken with poliomyelitis, which paralyzed him from the waist down. His struggle to overcome his handicap changed him from a condescending politician to a man who empathized with people in difficulty. He kept politically active by nominating Alfred E. Smith for the presidency at the Democratic Conventions in 1924 and 1928. In the latter year, he was elected Governor of New York. There, his relief measures to combat the Great Depression attracted national attention and won him the presidential nomination and the presidency in 1932.

As President, Roosevelt experimented to find some way out of the economic crisis. His programs of relief, recovery, and reform were often contradictory and hastily drawn. When faced with arguments over the proper course, he told his aides to work out differences even though they were irreconcilable. Yet, his program, called the New Deal, thrust the government permanently into economic life through agricultural price supports, bank regulation, the end of the gold standard, social security, federal housing aid, and labor union protection. This produced rancorous dissent from his opposition, but Roosevelt's warm, friendly voice broadcast over radio in his fireside chats won the vast majority of the public to his side. In foreign affairs, Roosevelt inaugurated the "Good Neighbor Policy" with Latin America, and tried to prepare the country for war when conflict became imminent in the late 1930s.

After the attack on Pearl Harbor in 1941, the President took a leading role meeting with world leaders to coordinate strategy and frame a postwar settlement. In this, he inherited President Wilson's idealism, upholding human freedom, national self-determination, and a new United Nations to solve disputes. Unfortunately, a cerebral hemorrhage ended his life before he could see the end of World War II.

HARRY S TRUMAN

May 8, 1884   *December 26, 1972*

President: April 12, 1945 - January 20, 1953

In contrast to his patrician predecessor, Harry S Truman appeared quite ordinary, speaking in a clipped and halting style, and was unknown. Consequently, he was underestimated. In fact, he was an extraordinary and feisty President, delivering forceful and peppery unprepared speeches, and becoming an international figure to be reckoned with. He made decisions quickly, based on his wide reading of history and biography, and on his experience.

Truman was born to a farming family in Missouri. A dispute involving two grandfathers, one named Solomon and the other named Shippe, resulted in using the initial S for his middle name. Because the family was poor, after attending public schools,

Truman went to work at a Kansas City newspaper in 1901, then as a railroad timekeeper, and finally as a helper in a bank, before returning to work the family farm from 1906 to 1917. When the United States entered World War I in 1917, Truman was commissioned an artillery lieutenant and saw action in France.

Upon his return, Truman became a partner in a haberdashery business, which failed in the brief postwar depression of 1921. Rather than declare bankruptcy, Truman gradually paid all his debtors in full. He then got involved in local Democratic politics, which was then controlled in Kansas City by the Thomas Pendergast machine. For his loyalty, he was elected Presiding Judge of Jackson County, the county's administrator, where he served with scrupulous honesty from 1922 to 1934. He also attended the Kansas City School of Law from 1923 to 1925. The combination of his political loyalty to the machine and his honest administration won him election to the Senate, where he served from 1935 to 1944. There, he loyally supported President Roosevelt's New Deal measures, and, during World War II, chaired with great effectiveness the Senate committee investigating wartime expenditures.

In 1944, Truman was unexpectedly chosen President Roosevelt's running mate, and was thus Vice President when Roosevelt died a few months after the inaugural. As President, Truman followed his predecessor's war policies by using the atomic bomb on Japan, but the subsequent threat from Stalin's Soviet Union led to the Truman Doctrine aiding Greece and Turkey, the Marshall Plan restoring Europe's economy, the Berlin Airlift breaking the Berlin Blockade, the creation of the NATO alliance, the provision of aid to underdeveloped nations, and the sending of troops to defend South Korea from a North Korean attack. At home, he expanded low cost housing, integrated the armed forces and federally supported schools, and refurbished the crumbling White House. Because he would have no other income upon retirement, he also obtained pensions for former Presidents.

President Truman's greatest political triumph came when he ran for election in 1948. Southerners objected to his civil rights stand, and radicals opposed his confrontation with the Soviet Union. The Democrats split into three parties, and most people were certain the Republican candidate would win. Surprisingly, Truman was elected by a decisive margin, the greatest political upset in American history.

DWIGHT DAVID EISENHOWER

October 14, 1890   *March 28, 1969*

President: January 20, 1953 - January 20, 1961

Dwight Eisenhower was born in Texas, but, in his first year, he moved with his poor family to Kansas, where he was graduated from high school in 1909. His family could not afford higher education for him, so he secured appointment to West Point two years later, graduating in the lower half of his class in 1915. During World War I, he commanded a tank-training program in Pennsylvania. In 1922, he went to the Panama Canal Zone for two years, returning to study at the General Staff Training School in Kansas and at the Army War College in Washington, D.C. From 1929 to 1933, he served in the office of the Assistant Secretary of War; then he was assigned to the Philippines as an assistant to General Douglas MacArthur until 1939. After the Pearl Harbor attack, he returned to Washington in various planning and operations positions.

Despite his lack of seniority, in 1942, Eisenhower was appointed Commander-in-Chief of the Allied Forces in North Africa. His background had given him broad experience in the staff and planning aspects of command, and he showed a capacity to lead troops and an ability to obtain cooperation without animosity from officers with opposing views and clashing personalities. His success there, in leading the assault on Sicily and Italy, in the invasion of France as the Supreme Commander of the Allied Expeditionary Force, and in the final European victory made him a popular hero. Through it all, however, Eisenhower never lost his modesty.

After World War II, Eisenhower became Army Chief of Staff, retiring in 1948 to become President of Columbia University. Two years later, however, President Truman called upon him to command the forces of the NATO alliance. The Republicans, nevertheless, looked to him as the military hero to win the presidency. He duly resigned in 1952, and won with an overwhelming popular vote.

As President, Eisenhower tried the same administrative methods he had used in the army. He delegated a great deal of authority to his Cabinet officers and staff to develop and implement policy. He studied their prepared proposals and and then made a decision based on them. He believed the President should not initiate policy, and he had no legislative program. Consequently, much of his domestic and foreign policy was a continuation of President Truman's despite the difference in party affiliation.

Eisenhower promoted building of Interstate Highways, ended the fighting in Korea, established SEATO in Southeast Asia, sent military advisors to South Vietnam, began the exploration of outer space, sent Federal troops to enforce the integration of schools in Little Rock, and encouraged science education. His infectious smile, seemingly guileless manner, and even the fractured syntax of his casual speech, endeared him to the American people. Although he presided over the nation in its period of greatest prosperity and military authority, in his farewell address, he warned of the growing power of the "military-industrial complex," which he believed would conspire to add unneeded expensive weaponry to the nation's arsenals.

JOHN FITZGERALD KENNEDY

May 29, 1917   *November 22, 1963*

President: January 20, 1961 - November 22, 1963

John F. Kennedy was the first Roman Catholic elected President. He was also the youngest person elected to that office, although not the youngest to enter it, since Theodore Roosevelt had been younger when he became President.

Kennedy was born in Massachusetts to a wealthy and politically ambitious family. His father, Joseph P. Kennedy, who gained a fortune in the stock market and as a financier, worked to have his eldest son, Joseph, Jr., chosen as the first Irish Catholic President. The elder Kennedy backed President Franklin Roosevelt and was appointed the first Chairman of the Securities and Exchange Commission, then Chairman of the Maritime Commission, and later Ambassador to Great Britain. Meanwhile, young John entered Harvard, briefly attending the London School of Economics in 1935, before graduating *cum laude* from Harvard in 1940. His senior thesis, *Why England Slept,* an analysis of Britain's reaction to growing Nazi power, was published the same year. When the United States entered World War II, he joined the Navy, commanding a PT boat in the Pacific, earning the Purple Heart, Navy, and Marine Corps medals. The death of his aviator brother, Joseph, Jr., in Europe during the war caused his father to transfer his presidential hopes to John.

Young Kennedy was elected to the House of Representatives in 1946, remaining there until elected a Senator from Massachusetts in 1952. In Congress, he supported most of President Truman's programs and President Eisenhower's foreign policy. In 1956, he published *Profiles in Courage,* a historical account of the careers of prominent Senators, which won the Pulitzer Prize. At the Democratic Convention that year, in a contest thrown open to the floor delegates, he nearly won the party's vice presidential nomination. His near miss led him to a four-year campaign for the presidency, and he won the Democratic nomination in 1960. The election was notable for the first series of televised debates between candidates for the office, in which the lesser known Kennedy impressed many with his oratorical eloquence, self-assurance, and intelligence. He won the election by a narrow margin of the popular vote.

Young, ambitious, a hard worker brimming with energy, Kennedy believed that the President should vigorously pursue the national interest and lead Congress. As President, he surrounded himself with intellectuals and visual and performing artists who viewed this era of their prominence and recognition by the handsome President as the "Camelot" of Arthurian legend. While Congress supported the President's programs on foreign aid, defense, and outer space exploration, it demurred on his ambitious social programs. His proposed tax cut and civil rights bills were pending at the time of his death. In foreign affairs, Kennedy's firmness compelled the Soviet Union to abandon Cuba as a missile base, and this led directly to the Nuclear Test Ban Treaty. He also inaugurated the Peace Corps and allowed American advisors in Vietnam to shoot back if fired upon. On a speechmaking tour in Dallas, Texas, the young President was fatally shot by Lee Harvey Oswald, leading to a national outpouring of grief.

LYNDON BAINES JOHNSON

August 27, 1908   *January 22, 1973*

President: November 22, 1963 - January 20, 1969

Born in a desperately poor farming area in southwestern Texas, Lyndon B. Johnson not only knew first-hand the effects of poverty on people, but also learned how to deal with the situation politically. His father was a highly regarded Democratic member of the Texas Legislature who worked with some success to alleviate his constituents' problems.

Facing limited opportunities, Johnson attended Southwest Texas State Teachers College, graduating in 1930, after which he taught public speaking in Houston until 1932. He got his first political break when he was hired by Democratic Congressman Richard M. Kleberg as his Congressional Secretary. Until 1935, he dealt with the Congressman's constituents and patronage, and also made important contacts in Washington, D.C. In 1935, he attended the Georgetown University Law School, but returned to Texas to become that state's Director of the National Youth Administration, one of President Franklin Roosevelt's New Deal agencies. In 1937, the death of Congressman James P. Buchanan gave Johnson the chance to run successfully for the open seat. A similar death, this time of Senator Morris Sheppard, in 1941, afforded Johnson the opportunity to run for that vacant seat, but this time, he lost. He remained in the House of Representatives until he won election to the Senate in 1948.

In the Senate, his talents won him the post of Democratic leader in 1953, where he was very effective. He was politically shrewd and persistent, but was also a conciliator. He had great powers of persuasion, and was not above threatening to disclose the indiscretions of a Senator to obtain his vote on an issue. He was, however, also egotistical and vindictive. Yet, he never lost his concern for the poor, and was chiefly responsible for the passage of the Civil Rights Acts of 1957 and 1960.

Johnson tried unsuccessfully to obtain the Democratic presidential nomination in 1960, losing to John F. Kennedy. He was selected the vice presidential candidate, however, despite the objections of Kennedy's close advisors. Kennedy won the election, and, after his assassination, Johnson became President.

As President, Johnson pledged to continue Kennedy's program, but he added to it a passionate commitment to eradicate poverty and to uphold the civil rights of blacks. His program, called the Great Society, included Federal aid to education, Medicare, Medicaid, the Voting Rights Act, Federal support of the arts and humanities, public broadcasting, safety standards for automobiles and highways, the Job Corps, and Head Start. In volume and effect, the effort can be compared only to Franklin Roosevelt's New Deal. The enactment and the promise of these programs secured President Johnson a landslide victory in the 1964 presidential election. Unfortunately, the war raging in Vietnam escalated, and he committed increasing numbers of American troops in an attempt to defeat Communist guerrillas there. This provoked such opposition and civil unrest at home that, in 1968, the man who had won the presidency by an overwhelming landslide four years earlier was compelled to state that he would not run again.

RICHARD MILHOUS NIXON

January 9, 1913   *April 22, 1994*

President: January 20, 1969 - August 9, 1974

Richard Nixon elicited more undying loyalty, and more implacable hatred, than most American political figures. To some, he represented the embodiment of middle class values in an unsettling era, with the added virtues of intelligence and perseverance. To others, he was an opportunist, who was shifty, righteous, and defensive. With opinions about him poles apart, perhaps it is not a cause for wonder that this man rose to be President of the United States only to become the first to resign from that office in disgrace.

Born in California to a Quaker family who brought him up frugally, Richard Nixon became a lonely and solemn young man who had learned the virtues of work, discipline, and ambition. He graduated from Whittier College in 1934, and from Duke University Law School in 1937. He returned to California to practice law. After the outbreak of World War II, Nixon briefly served in the Office of Price Administration in 1942, but resigned to join the Navy. After his service in the South Pacific, he was discharged with the rank of Lieutenant Commander.

With the aid of his war record, he won election to Congress as a Republican in 1946. There, he gained national attention as a member of the House Un-American Activities Committee. He badgered Alger Hiss, an esteemed New Dealer, to show that he once had Communist ties. Nixon received plaudits for his performance from many people, but was also vilified for his methods by New Deal supporters. In 1950, he won election to the Senate by labelling his opponent a Communist sympathizer, a tactic which solidified his supporters behind him and his opponents against him.

At the Republican Convention in 1952, Nixon was named Eisenhower's vice presidential candidate. He served President Eisenhower loyally, and obtained his endorsement for the Republican presidential nomination in 1960, but was defeated by John F. Kennedy. Nixon returned to California, and ran unsuccessfully for Governor there in 1962. He petulantly announced his retirement from politics, and moved to New York to practice law.

Following the Republican landslide defeat in 1964, Nixon became the only nationally known Republican to campaign for the party's state and local nominees throughout the country and, in gratitude, they afforded him the presidential nomination in 1968. The nation, torn by the conflict in Vietnam, narrowly elected Nixon President. As President, Nixon's strong point was foreign affairs. He eventually deescalated the American involvement in Vietnam, visited both China and the Soviet Union to ease tensions with the United States, and began the process of bringing peace in the Middle East. In his reelection campaign in 1972, some White House aides condoned placing hidden microphones in the Democratic Headquarters at the Watergate complex in Washington. After investigation by Senate and House committees, proof was offered that the President tried to prevent his aides' arrest, thus committing a crime and violating President Washington's standard of republican virtue. After the House Judiciary Committee voted to recommend impeachment of the President to the full House, President Nixon resigned.

GERALD RUDOLPH FORD

July 14, 1913   - - - -

President: August 9, 1974 - January 20, 1977

When Leslie King, Jr. was born in Nebraska, no one suspected that he would become the first President to hold the office without winning a nationwide election, and that his name would be Gerald Ford. At the age of two, his parents were divorced. His mother then moved with him to Michigan, where she married Gerald Rudolph Ford, who adopted her son and gave him his name.

The newly named Gerald Ford attended the University of Michigan, playing on the varsity football team before graduating from there in 1935. After graduating from Yale Law School in 1941, he returned to Michigan to practice law. After the Pearl Harbor attack, he joined the Navy in 1942, serving in the Pacific. He left in 1946 with the rank of Lieutenant Commander. For a time, while practicing law, the handsome and athletic young man earned some money posing as an advertising model.

In 1948, Gerald Ford won election to Congress as a Republican, serving without interruption for twenty-five years. In the House of Representatives, he was not regarded as a leader of national stature, but he had a likable personality. He was honest, and he never seemed to take offense. He may have disagreed with other Congressmen over policy and principle, but he did not make that a cause for personal enmity. Because of his longevity in office and his personality, Ford served as the Republican Leader of the House in his last eight years there. Normally, if the majority of Representatives were Republicans, he would have served as Speaker of the House, the only office of national significance to which he aspired. The continued Democratic dominance of that body, however, assured him that his wish would never be fulfilled.

In 1973, Vice President Spiro Agnew resigned after admitting he had accepted bribes years earlier as a government official in Maryland. Under the Twenty-fifth Amendment, ratified in 1967, the President nominates a person to fill a vice presidential vacancy; the nominee must then be confirmed by a majority vote of both houses of Congress. The affable Ford appeared to be President Nixon's best choice, since members of both parties liked him. Ford, knowing he could never be Speaker, agreed to take the job. When President Nixon resigned the following year, Gerald Ford took over the office without having won a national election. He nominated Nelson Rockefeller, the former Governor of New York, for Vice President, and the nation, for the first time, had two national leaders who were never elected to their offices.

President Ford was modest about his attainments, and even became the butt of jokes for being physically clumsy, which he took with good humor. He tried to calm the country by pardoning President Nixon for any crimes he may have committed, but this outraged many Americans. The celebration of the 200th anniversary of American independence in 1976, however, did help restore the faith of many people in their governmental institutions. The biggest crisis President Ford faced was inflation, caused in large part by an oil embargo imposed by Arab oil suppliers. The President vetoed bills establishing economic controls as too costly. Wanting to be elected in his own right, he obtained the Republican nomination for President in 1976 over the vigorous opposition of Ronald Reagan of California, only to lose the election.

JIMMY CARTER

October 1, 1924   - - - -

President: January 20, 1977 - January 20, 1981

Born James Earl Carter, Jr., but preferring to be called by the friendly and folksy name of Jimmy, this son of rural Georgia was not always what he seemed. His parents were leading citizens of their small town, owning a peanut farm, the local peanut warehouse, and the cotton gin. Intelligent and diligent, young Carter showed an interest in science and technology.

Consequently, Carter studied at Georgia Tech, and then entered the Naval Academy at Annapolis. After graduation, he entered the Navy's nuclear submarine program as an aide to Admiral Hyman Rickover, the father of the nuclear submarine. While in the Navy, he also studied nuclear physics at Union College in Schenectady, New York. The simple Georgia farmboy had become a nuclear engineer.

With the death of his father in 1953, Carter decided to leave the Navy to return to Georgia and take over the family businesses. There, he became a "born again" fundamentalist Baptist, serving as a deacon of his local church and as a Sunday School teacher. His interest in education led him to service on his local public school board, which, in turn, led him into political life. He was elected as a Democrat to the State Senate, tried unsuccessfully to run for Governor in 1966, but did win the governorship in 1970. At the completion of his term, he began a campaign to win the presidency despite the fact that he was virtually unknown outside Georgia.

In the mid-1970s, in the wake of President Nixon's resignation and his pardon by President Ford, the people saw Jimmy Carter as the only man wanting the presidency who lacked experience in the nation's capital and was not tainted by the recent Watergate scandals. His simple, unassuming manner and his preachy piety were favorably received. Carter thus won the Democratic nomination for President, and won the election by a narrow popular vote.

As President, Carter had no overall vision or direction, and was often bogged down in detail. Since he and his staff had no Washington experience, the White House was often at odds with Congress. Carter did make human rights a goal in foreign affairs. The President also played a major role in mediating a peace treaty between Egypt and Israel, the first such treaty in the war between Israel and any of its Arab neighbors. He also espoused a treaty returning the Panama Canal Zone to full Panamanian sovereignty in the year 2000. At home, President Carter ended regulation of airlines, trucks, railroads, and banks, contending that the economy was overregulated.

President Carter's inability to solve the problems of inflation and oil supply, coupled with the capture of American diplomats as hostages in Iran following an Islamic revolution there, and his pessimistic insistence that there was a national malaise in the country, did not appeal to voters. Although the Democrats nominated him for President again, he lost his bid for reelection. The public announcement from Iran that the American hostages had been released came hours after he left the presidency.

RONALD WILSON REAGAN

February 6, 1911   - - - -

President: January 20, 1981 - January 20, 1989

The life of Ronald Reagan is full of contradictions. He was first a Democrat casting his first four presidential votes for Franklin Roosevelt, and then became a Republican. He was the leader of a labor union (the Screen Actors Guild) who led a successful strike, who, as President, broke the strike of the Professional Air Traffic Controllers Organization. He was a man who advocated traditional family values, but became the first President who had divorced and remarried. He was a man who espoused cutting government spending, but he retired from the presidency leaving the largest government deficit in history. He was a man who expressed total opposition to the Soviet Union and Communism as the embodiment of evil, yet became the man who eased tensions between the Soviet Union and the United States and signed the first nuclear arms reduction agreement with that country. He was born poor, but became the friend of the rich. He had a relaxed, genial personality, but displayed a withering anger when crossed. He preferred to set general policy directions and let others carry them out, but he strengthened presidential authority.

Ronald Reagan was born to a poor Illinois family. In 1932, he graduated from Eureka College, and then spent five years as a radio sports announcer in Des Moines, Iowa. In 1937, he moved to Hollywood, where his boyish good looks got him acting jobs playing supporting "good guy" roles. He was never a star. In World War II, as a Captain in the Army Air Force, he spent most of the time narrating training films. After the war, his acting career waned, and he became a spokesman for the General Electric Company.

In 1964, for the first time, he publicly supported the Republican candidate opposed to the Democrat, President Lyndon Johnson, largely because he believed high taxation for social programs would erode his hard-won wealth. Wealthy friends convinced him to run for Governor of California in 1966, and he won, serving two terms. Following his service there, he became the spokesman for Republicans who wanted to reduce government taxation and regulation of business. An unsuccessful attempt to win the Republican presidential nomination in 1976 was followed by a successful campaign in 1980 and election to the presidency.

As President, Reagan made good on his promise to reduce taxation, but he also increased military spending greatly. Rivalry among the Middle Eastern countries made the cost of oil and gas cheaper, thus facilitating economic growth with reduced inflation. The President also restored pride in the country and its power through the successful invasion of the Caribbean island nation of Grenada after a Marxist coup there threatened the lives of American medical students. His support of rebels against the revolutionary Sandinista government of Nicaragua, the ill-fated stationing of American troops in war-torn Beirut, and the naval patrol of the Persian Gulf, however, were met with a more ambivalent response. The President, however, always radiating optimism, sure in his abilities to communicate his message to the American people, and with a boyish charm despite his advanced age, left the presidency with his popularity as high as when he entered it.

GEORGE HERBERT WALKER BUSH

June 12, 1924   - - - -

President: January 20, 1989 - *January 20, 1993*

George Bush came to the Presidency with a greater preparation than most of his predecessors. He was born in Massachusetts to a wealthy family.   His father, Prescott Bush, was a Wall Street banker and, after 1952, served as a Republican United States Senator from Connecticut. Young Bush attended Phillips Academy in Andover, from which he graduated in 1942.

In 1942, on his eighteenth birthday, he volunteered for the Navy in World War II, became its youngest pilot, and completed 57 combat missions flying torpedo bombers in the Pacific before being shot down by the Japanese in 1944. For his deeds, he received three air medals and the Distinguished Flying Cross.

In 1945, he entered Yale University and married. He became

captain of the varsity baseball team. After graduation in 1948, he refused to take a job set aside for him in the Wall Street banking firm. Receiving financial help from his uncle, he moved to Texas, and became an equipment and sales clerk, and later a salesman, for the International Derrick and Equipment Company. In 1951, he cofounded the Bush-Overbay Development Company to buy mineral rights and explore for oil, and founded the Zapata Petroleum Corporation for oil drilling in 1953. As President and cofounder of the Zapata Offshore Company, which pioneered the use of offshore drilling equipment, Bush earned his own fortune.

In 1964, he ran for the Senate as a Republican in Texas, but he lost in the midst of the Democratic landslide that year. Two years later, he ran for the House of Representatives and won. In Congress, he defended the oil interests of Houston, but also voted for open housing for blacks. His abilities came to the notice of President Nixon, who asked him to run for the Senate in 1970, but, once again, he lost.

President Nixon, as a reward, named him American Ambassador to the United Nations, which first brought Bush to national attention. His continued loyalty to the President during the turmoil of the Watergate affair led President Nixon to push through the election of Bush as Chairman of the Republican National Committee in 1973. In 1974, President Ford put him in charge of the American liaison office in China, a post that existed prior to the official recognition of the Communist regime there. His capability, circumspection, consideration, and loyalty in all these posts led to his appointment as Director of the Central Intelligence Agency in 1976.

In 1980, Bush ran for the Republican presidential nomination, but lost to Ronald Reagan. Despite calling Reagan's economic plan, "voodoo economics," he became his Vice Presidential candidate. In office, Bush showed some firmness of character and a sense of courtesy, trying to please and to paper over disagreements. In 1988, his record and character won him the Republican presidential nomination. In a bitter campaign, he ran on his record of loyalty and experience, promised no new taxes, and won handily.

Bush's major accomplishments came in the field of foreign affairs. Notably, when Iraqi forces overran Kuwait, he organized an international coalition with the blessings of the United Nations and of Congress to expel them. The Cold War finally ended in 1991 when the Soviet Union collapsed. However, the increasing financial deficit caused him to break his pledge not to raise taxes, and that cost him reelection in 1992.

WILLIAM JEFFERSON CLINTON

August 19, 1946   - - - -

President: January 20, 1993 - - - - -

William Jefferson Clinton's beginnings in life were among the least promising for anyone aspiring to be president. Born in Arkansas, he was originally named William Jefferson Blythe. His father, a traveling salesman, was killed in an automobile accident before his birth. His mother eventually was remarried, to Roger Clinton, and, at age 16, the youngster changed his last name to Clinton. His stepfather, however, was an abusive drunkard, and the strapping lad had to defend his mother. Young Clinton, highly intelligent, joined the Boys' Republic youth group. On an outing with them to Washington, D.C., he met President Kennedy, shaking his hand. This inspired him to go into public service, and to specialize in foreign affairs.

He was educated at Georgetown University in Washington,

majoring in international affairs and graduated in 1968. He received a Rhodes scholarship to attend Oxford University from 1968 to 1970. At the time, the Vietnam War was raging. Clinton concluded that the war was wrong and tried to avoid the draft. He received a deferment, first as a student, and then because his draft number was too high for the lottery system then in effect. As a student, Clinton readily made friends, and kept a file of their names and addresses. He enjoyed discussing policy issues with them. He then attended Yale University Law School, graduating in 1973. There he met, and eventually married Hillary Rodham, with whom he shared similar interests. While there, he also became politically active by joining the 1972 presidential campaign of Democrat George McGovern, who opposed the Vietnam War, against Richard Nixon.

Upon graduation from Yale, he became a professor at the University of Arkansas, while simultaneously opening up a law practice. In 1976, he ran for public office for the first time, successfully winning the post of Arkansas Attorney General. In 1978, Clinton, calling himself by the more familiar first name of Bill rather than the more formal William, won the governorship of Arkansas. Still young, and highly intelligent, he saw himself as having all the answers and provoked great opposition in the state's legislative bodies trying to push through his programs without compromise. The resulting lack of progress led to his losing reelection. Learning his lesson, he ran again in 1982, this time winning. He kept on winning each time he ran. Now, he was willing to compromise on his programs, but when only part of what he wanted was enacted, he would return again and again until, in time, all his ideas became law.

Clinton's intelligence and abilities came to the attention of his fellow governors, who elected him Chairman of the National Governors Association in 1986 and 1987. He was also a leader of the Democratic Leadership Council from 1990 to 1991. Despite coming from a small state, Clinton was looked upon by many Democrats as a potential candidate for the presidency in 1992.

Receiving the Democratic nomination in 1992, Clinton promised to better the economy and to change long-held government practices. He won by a narrow margin, but his bold program of health reform was blocked by Congress. Despite overturning restrictions on abortion, easing conditions to register to vote, reducing the deficit, brokering peace between Palestinians and Israelis, and pushing through the North American Free Trade Association, failure to adequately address the questions of welfare, and floundering in the Somalian and Bosnian civil wars led to a disenchantment with his leadership.

THE PRESIDENTS BEFORE
GEORGE WASHINGTON

The title of President of the United States was not new when George Washington was elected to the post. It had its origins in the First Continental Congress in 1774 which gave a presidential title to the man who wielded the gavel and presided over its meetings. With the adoption of the Articles of Confederation on November 15, 1777, and its subsequent ratification on March 1, 1781, the Second Continental Congress became officially The United States of America in Congress Assembled, and its presiding officer was called the President of the United States of America in Congress Assembled. This President had no power other than to preside over the meetings of the Congress. In fact, Congressmen were appointed by their respective State Legislatures and their President was then chosen by the members of Congress from among themselves. The Constitutional Convention in 1787, wishing to preserve the old terminology while creating a new form of government, maintained the title of Congress for the Federal Legislature and called the new chief executive by the old title of President of the United States. These, then, are the men who served as Presidents before George Washington:

The First Continental Congress:

Peyton Randolph of Virginia, September 5, 1774 - October 5, 1774 (resigned)
Henry Middleton of South Carolina, October 5 - 22, 1774

The Second Continental Congress:

Peyton Randolph of Virginia, May 10 - 24, 1775
John Hancock of Massachusetts, May 24, 1775 - November 1, 1777
Henry Laurens of South Carolina, November 1, 1777 - December 10, 1778

John Jay of New York, December 10, 1778 - September 28, 1779
Samuel Huntington of Connecticut, September 28, 1779 - March 1, 1781

The United States of America in Congress Assembled:

Samuel Huntington of Connecticut, March 1 - July 10, 1781
Thomas McKean of Delaware, July 10 - November 5, 1781
John Hanson of Maryland, November 5, 1781 - November 4, 1782
Elias Boudinot of New Jersey, November 4, 1782 - November 3, 1783
Thomas Mifflin of Pennsylvania, November 3, 1783 - November 30, 1784
Richard Henry Lee of Virginia, November 30, 1784 - November 23, 1785
John Hancock of Massachusetts, November 23, 1785 - May 29, 1786 (resigned)
Nathaniel Gorham of Massachusetts, June 6, 1786 - February 2, 1787
Arthur St. Clair of Pennsylvania, February 2, 1787 - January 22, 1788
Cyrus Griffin of Virginia, January 22, 1788 - March 2, 1789

THE ELECTORAL COLLEGE AND PRESIDENTIAL ELECTIONS

Most Americans would find it surprising to learn that the people do not directly elect the President of the United States. When they go into a voting booth to choose the person they wish to occupy the White House for the ensuing four years, they are not electing the President. They are choosing a number of Electors who, in turn, will cast their own ballots for President.

The Electoral College was framed by the Constitutional Convention in 1787. James Madison's Virginia Plan had first proposed that the President be elected by Congress for seven years and be ineligible for reelection. Many delegates, however, believed that this mode of election made the President too dependent on Congress, thus violating the principle of the separation of powers among the legislative, executive, and judicial authorities. Gouverneur Morris and James Wilson suggested that the President be elected by the people, but others thought that the President might pander to mob rule or manipulate the populace to establish a tyranny. They believed, moreover, that the people would not know the best candidates for the job. Other suggestions for election included a choice made by Governors, or by Electors appointed by State Legislatures, but no method proposed seemed to satisfy the delegates.

The matter was not resolved until near the end of the Convention in the committee dealing with postponed matters chaired by David Brearley. By the proposed method, which the Convention adopted, each State Legislature decided the manner in which the Electors would be chosen. The number of Electors in each state would be equal to the number of its Representatives plus Senators, but Electors were forbidden to be members of Congress or Federal office holders. The Electors were to meet in their respective state capitals and mark two names on a ballot, one of which had to be from a state other than their own. The ballots would then be sent to the Federal capital and counted by the President of the Senate before a joint session of Congress. The person having the most votes, provided that number was a majority, would become President. If two persons were tied and each had a majority, the House of Representatives would then make the choice between them, but the Representatives would not vote as individuals; they would vote by state, all the Representatives from one state casting one collective vote. If no person had a majority of the Electoral College vote, the House of Representatives would make the choice from among the five highest vote getters using the same voting rules. The person having the second highest number of Electoral votes would become the Vice President, but, if there were a tie, the Senate would choose between them.

Almost everyone at the Convention knew that George Washington would be elected President by the Electoral College, but they were not sure about his successors. No political parties existed at the time, and the Convention's delegates believed that the Electors would most often not come up with the name of a person who could achieve a majority of their votes. They were thus convinced that the Electoral College would serve as a nominating body, thus leaving the actual choice to the House of Representatives voting by state.

The rise of political parties changed that expectation. In 1796, it led to the election of a President from one party, the Federalist, John Adams, and a Vice President from another, the Republican, Thomas Jefferson. Four years later, the system led to an Electoral College tie between two Republicans, Thomas Jefferson, who was the presidential candidate, and Aaron Burr, who had been slated for Vice President. The choice fell to the House of Representatives voting by state. There was a deadlock until the thirty-sixth ballot.

To prevent such things from happening again, the Twelfth Amendment to the Constitution was added in 1804. Henceforward, the Electors would cast two ballots, one for President and one for Vice President. If no one received a majority of the Electoral College vote, then the House of Representatives voting by state would choose from among the three highest vote getters. Except for these changes, the original system remained in place, and still does to this day.

Almost all further modifications in the election of the President came about through law and custom. For instance, the State Legislature decides how the Electors from its state will be chosen. In the earliest elections, most Legislatures chose the Electors directly. As the democratic idea grew in the nineteenth century, the Legislatures, one by one, permitted the people to elect the Electors; the last holdout was South Carolina which still had its Legislature appointing its Electors as late as 1860.

By 1824, the popular vote for Electors became a significant factor in choosing the President. In that year, Andrew Jackson won the popular vote (153,544) over John Quincy Adams (108,740), and had the most Electoral votes (99 to 84). Since others were in the race, however, neither man received a majority in the Electoral College, and, for the second time, the House of Representatives had to make the choice voting by state. On the first ballot, the Representatives surprisingly voted to elect Adams, who had come in second in both the popular and Electoral vote.

From that time onward, political leaders have made it a cardinal rule to avoid at all costs giving the choice of the presidency to the House of Representatives. To be certain that one person receives an Electoral College majority, the choice had to be limited. It meant that the political parties could not afford to organize around only one state, group of states, or one section of the country, but had to appeal to the nation at large. It also meant that the political parties could not be structured around an ideology that would appeal to only a minority of the electorate. All points of view in the country had to be encompassed within a large political party to assure that a majority vote in the Electoral College would be achieved. Two major parties were thus created. The task of the major parties was to reconcile any differences in points of view among its members and appeal to a majority of the voters in each state to choose a majority of the Electoral College to elect the candidate.

It was for this purpose that the national political party convention was instituted. In 1831, the Antimasonic Party held the first party convention, and the National Republicans and the Democrats quickly followed. This development was ostensibly a democratization of the nominating process. Instead of a few political leaders meeting in caucus in a state or in Congress suggesting the names of candidates as they did heretofore, now a nation wide meeting of delegates chosen by state conventions representing a broad range of people would deliberate among themselves and nominate a candidate. The convention would also adopt a platform, which presumably expressed the principles and program of the party. In reality, as it developed over the years, the platform of each party was expressed in general, and sometimes contradictory, terms in order to smooth over differences in points of view. This would help unite the party behind its chosen candidate. If this effort failed, as it did among the Democrats in 1860 and 1948, and among the Republicans in 1912, the party would split and jeopardize its candidate's election. As the system has developed, two non-ideological mass parties compete to garner the popular vote, thus insuring that one of them will obtain a majority in the Electoral College.

To complete the picture, the organization of each national party in each state must secure the vote of the Electors. Since the voters do not elect a President, but elect Electors, each state party nominates a full slate of candidates for Electors. Those chosen are party regulars whose loyalty is unquestioned. Each nominee for the post is pledged, if elected, to cast his ballot for the candidate of his party for President and for Vice President. To further insure that the House of Representatives will not ultimately make the choice of the chief executive, each state requires by law that the nominees for Electors of each party run as a slate, and that an entire slate is elected throughout the state.

It is possible that the popular vote for President in a few states could be close, and in other states could be overwhelmingly for one candidate, thus producing a decision where one candidate gets a majority of the popular vote while the other wins a majority of the Electoral College. This happened in 1888 when Grover Cleveland narrowly won the popular vote over Benjamin Harrison (5,537,857 to 5,477,129), but lost the Electoral vote (168 to 233), which made Harrison President.

Moreover, it is possible for an Elector to violate his pledge and not vote for the candidate of his party. In 1956, one Democratic Elector in Alabama refused to vote for Adlai E. Stevenson, his party's presidential nominee, and in 1960, Senator Harry F. Byrd of Virginia received fifteen Electoral votes even though he had not been nominated by any party. Similarly, in 1972, one Virginia Elector voted for John Hospers of Oregon for President, and four years later, one Washington Elector cast his ballot for Ronald Reagan of California. In 1988, Senator Lloyd Bentsen of Texas received one Electoral vote. To prevent such action, party leaders isolate such Electors, refusing to consider them for any future elected or appointed office, and will use them as an example of what might happen to others who dare follow in their path.

Since the last decade of the nineteenth century, the movement to secure nomination of state and local candidates through primary elections has grown. In the twentieth century, the movement has encompassed delegates to the national party conventions, and the number of states holding primary elections for national party convention delegates has also increased. By the 1970s, this movement greatly diminished the role of the political leaders and even of the convention itself. Most often, voters in each party select a majority of delegates pledged to nominate one candidate before the convention meets. Yet, the convention remains the nominating institution of last resort if no one obtains a majority of delegates, and it still retains the role of forming the platform to smooth over the varying points of view of the delegates.

The last change, a minor one to be sure, in the election of the President occurred with the passage of the Twenty-third Amendment in 1961, which gives voters in the District of Columbia a voice in the selection. By its terms, the District is entitled to a number of Electors equal to the number in the least populous state, and these are to be chosen as Congress directs. As in the states, Congress has decreed that the District's Electors be elected by the people and that an entire slate be chosen at once.

There have been suggestions made to abolish the Electoral College and that the President be elected directly by the people as Gouverneur Morris wanted. Those who make this demand point to the unfair outcome of the 1888 election, the added weight given the small states in apportioning the number of Electors, the possibility that Electors will not cast their ballot for their party's candidate, the unfairness of electing the Electors by slate, and the general undemocratic nature of it all.

On the other hand, there are those who point out the advantages of the Electoral College. They say that it brings certainty to the election of the President, especially if the popular vote is close. In addition, in this electronic age, it makes the results of the presidential election known within hours, rather than fostering a long wait for the counting of every popular vote. By giving added weight to the smaller states, the system forces presidential candidates to pay attention to a wide variety of issues across the nation, rather than only those of moment to the most populous states. Above all, the Electoral College, with its requirement of a majority vote for election and the threat of throwing the choice to the uncertain hands of the House of Representatives if a majority is not achieved, fosters the creation of the stable, non-ideological national two party system, rather than an ideologically ordered multi-party one, which might have been expected in such an extensive country with its variety of interests.

THE LENGTH OF A
PRESIDENTIAL TERM

When the Constitution was first written in 1787, there was a provision that the President of the United States be elected for a four year term without a bar to reelection. It did not specify, however, when that term would begin or end.

The first Congress under the new Constitution convened in New York City on March 4, 1789, and the Electoral votes unanimously choosing George Washington as the first President were counted and certified afterward. It took a full 57 days after Congress convened for Washington to receive the official notification of his election and for him to travel from Virginia to New York for his inaugural on April 30, 1789. Although the administration of the executive branch of the government thus began in April, Washington's second inaugural, in 1793, took place on March 4th, the anniversary of the initial meeting of the first Congress. Therefore, President Washington's first term was 57 days short of four years, and March 4th became the inauguration day for almost a century and a half.

The first time a date appears in the Constitution for the beginning of a presidential term occurs in the Twelfth Amendment, ratified in 1804. This codified the March 4th date.

By the twentieth century, the increased swiftness of communication and travel made the four month wait between the popular election and the inauguration of the President cumbersome. By 1932, during the Great Depression, the populace felt that the long delay in ending the discredited Hoover administration and starting a new term in the midst of an economic crisis of Olympian proportions was actually harmful. That year, the Twentieth Amendment passed Congress and was ratified in 1933. This established January 3rd as the date for the commencement of a new Congress and it set the new presidential inaugural date at January 20th. It also specified that the presidential term would begin at noon on that day, instead of at the completion of oath by the new President as had hitherto been the custom. Since Franklin Roosevelt had already been elected in 1932 and inaugurated in 1933, his first term was cut short by 43 days. Because he was reelected in 1936 and inaugurated on January 20, 1937, the changed date had no practical impact on presidential policy.

Although the Constitution originally placed no bar on the reelection of the President, George Washington felt that two terms should be the maximum for any man, and he declined to run again. Thomas Jefferson agreed with him, and decided to retire from the presidency after the completion of his second term as well. By following Washington's example, Jefferson reinforced an unwritten precedent limiting a President to a maximum of two terms.

This precedent held until 1940. Then, Franklin Roosevelt, faced with the danger to the country of war in both Europe and the Pacific, decided to run for a third term. His electoral victory that year, and in 1944, when the United States was in the midst of fighting World War II, shattered the unwritten two-term precedent.

Despite Roosevelt's overwhelming popularity at that time, many resented the President's action and wished to see the two-term precedent restored. Consequently, in 1951, the Twenty-second Amendment was added to the Constitution. It forbids anyone to be President more than twice, although it exempted the incumbent at the time, Harry S Truman, from the ban. Truman, however, chose not to run again.

A President may serve less than the mandated four years in several ways. Death in office is the most common reason for a short term. This happened to William Henry Harrison, Zachary Taylor, Abraham Lincoln, James A. Garfield, William McKinley, Warren G. Harding, Franklin Roosevelt, and John F. Kennedy. A much less common reason is resignation from office. Only one President, Richard Nixon, resigned from the presidency. In addition, a President may be removed from office upon conviction in a trial in the Senate following impeachment by the House of Representatives. Only one President, Andrew Johnson, was ever impeached, but he was not convicted and served his term. Of course, a Vice President, upon assuming the Presidency, completes the term to which his predecessor was elected, thus also serving less than four years. This happened to John Tyler, Millard Fillmore, Andrew Johnson, Chester A. Arthur, Theodore Roosevelt, Calvin Coolidge, Harry S Truman, Lyndon B. Johnson, and Gerald Ford. Of course, four of these men, Roosevelt, Coolidge, Truman, and Lyndon Johnson, successfully gained election to four-year terms on their own.

PRESIDENTIAL ELECTIONS
SINCE 1789

In this list of candidates for President through the years, the winner is displayed in capital letters, and the losers are printed in both upper and lower case lettering. In the first three elections, only the candidates receiving the two highest Electoral votes are listed. After that, those listed before the election of 1824 received at least one Electoral vote. Those listed from the election of 1824 onward received at least one percent of the popular vote. Political parties are appended to the names of each candidate, except for the first two elections when no political designation existed. There might be some confusion in the use of the name "Republican" up to 1824 and from 1856 onward. The first Republican Party was founded by Thomas Jefferson, and broke into two factions, the Democratic Republicans, which soon became the Democrats, and the National Republicans, which became the Whigs. The second Republican Party was formed by antislavery Whigs and Democrats. In the case of third or fourth parties, the official name is used, and, if there is a popular nickname for any of these parties, it appears in parentheses following the official name.

Date	*Candidates*	*Parties*
1789	GEORGE WASHINGTON	
	John Adams	
1792	GEORGE WASHINGTON	
	John Adams	
1796	JOHN ADAMS	Federalist
	Thomas Jefferson	Republican

1800	THOMAS JEFFERSON	Republican
	Aaron Burr	Republican
	John Adams	Federalist
	Charles C. Pinckney	Federalist
	John Jay	Federalist
1804	THOMAS JEFFERSON	Republican
	Charles C. Pinckney	Federalist
1808	JAMES MADISON	Republican
	Charles C. Pinckney	Federalist
	George Clinton	Republican
1812	JAMES MADISON	Republican
	DeWitt Clinton	Federalist
1816	JAMES MONROE	Republican
	Rufus King	Federalist
1820	JAMES MONROE	Republican
	John Quincy Adams	Republican
1824	JOHN QUINCY ADAMS	Republican
	Andrew Jackson	Republican
	William H. Crawford	Republican
	Henry Clay	Republican
1828	ANDREW JACKSON	Democratic Republican
	John Quincy Adams	National Republican
1832	ANDREW JACKSON	Democratic
	Henry Clay	National Republican
	William Wirt	Anti-Masonic
	John Floyd	National Republican
1836	MARTIN VAN BUREN	Democratic
	William Henry Harrison	Whig
	Hugh L. White	Whig
	Daniel Webster	Whig
	W.P. Mangum	Whig
1840	WILLIAM HENRY HARRISON	Whig
	Martin Van Buren	Democratic

1844	JAMES K. POLK	Democratic
	Henry Clay	Whig
	James G. Birney	Liberty
1848	ZACHARY TAYLOR	Whig
	Lewis Cass	Democratic
	Martin Van Buren	Free Soil
1852	FRANKLIN PIERCE	Democratic
	Winfield Scott	Whig
	John P. Hale	Free Soil
1856	JAMES BUCHANAN	Democratic
	John C. Fremont	Republican
	Millard Fillmore	American (Know-Nothing)
1860	ABRAHAM LINCOLN	Republican
	Stephen A. Douglas	Democratic
	John C. Breckinridge	Democratic
	John Bell	Constitutional Union
1864	ABRAHAM LINCOLN	Union
	George B. McClellan	Democratic
1868	ULYSSES S. GRANT	Republican
	Horatio Seymour	Democratic
1872	ULYSSES S. GRANT	Republican
	Horace Greeley	Democratic
1876	RUTHERFORD B. HAYES	Republican
	Samuel J. Tilden	Democratic
1880	JAMES A. GARFIELD	Republican
	Winfield S. Hancock	Democratic
	James B. Weaver	Greenback-Labor
1884	GROVER CLEVELAND	Democratic
	James G. Blaine	Republican
	Benjamin F. Butler	Greenback-Labor
	John P. St. John	Prohibition

1888	BENJAMIN HARRISON	Republican
	Grover Cleveland	Democratic
	Clinton B. Fisk	Prohibition
	Anson J. Streeter	Union Labor
1892	GROVER CLEVELAND	Democratic
	Benjamin Harrison	Republican
	James B. Weaver	People's (Populist)
	John Bidwell	Prohibition
1896	WILLIAM McKINLEY	Republican
	William Jennings Bryan	Democratic; People's
1900	WILLIAM McKINLEY	Republican
	William Jennings Bryan	Democratic
	John C. Wooley	Prohibition
1904	THEODORE ROOSEVELT	Republican
	Alton B. Parker	Democratic
	Eugene V. Debs	Socialist
	Silas C. Swallow	Prohibition
1908	WILLIAM HOWARD TAFT	Republican
	William Jennings Bryan	Democratic
	Eugene V. Debs	Socialist
	Eugene W. Chafin	Prohibition
1912	WOODROW WILSON	Democratic
	Theodore Roosevelt	Progressive (Bull Moose)
	William Howard Taft	Republican
	Eugene V. Debs	Socialist
	Eugene W. Chafin	Prohibition
1916	WOODROW WILSON	Democratic
	Charles Evans Hughes	Republican
	A.L. Benson	Socialist
	J. Frank Hanley	Prohibition
1920	WARREN G. HARDING	Republican
	James N. Cox	Democratic
	Eugene V. Debs	Socialist
	P.P. Christensen	Farmer-Labor

1924	CALVIN COOLIDGE	Republican
	John W. Davis	Democratic
	Robert M. La Follette	Progressive
1928	HERBERT C. HOOVER	Republican
	Alfred E. Smith	Democratic
1932	FRANKLIN D. ROOSEVELT	Democratic
	Herbert C. Hoover	Republican
	Norman Thomas	Socialist
1936	FRANKLIN D. ROOSEVELT	Democratic
	Alfred M. Landon	Republican
	William Lemke	Union
1940	FRANKLIN D. ROOSEVELT	Democratic
	Wendell L. Willkie	Republican
1944	FRANKLIN D. ROOSEVELT	Democratic
	Thomas E. Dewey	Republican
1948	HARRY S TRUMAN	Democratic
	Thomas E. Dewey	Republican
	J. Strom Thurmond	States' Rights (Dixiecrat)
	Henry A. Wallace	Progressive
1952	DWIGHT D. EISENHOWER	Republican
	Adlai E. Stevenson	Democratic
1956	DWIGHT D. EISENHOWER	Republican
	Adlai E. Stevenson	Democratic
1960	JOHN F. KENNEDY	Democratic
	Richard M. Nixon	Republican
1964	LYNDON B. JOHNSON	Democratic
	Barry M. Goldwater	Republican
1968	RICHARD M. NIXON	Republican
	Hubert H. Humphrey	Democratic
	George C. Wallace	American Independent

1972	RICHARD M. NIXON	Republican
	George S. McGovern	Democratic

1976	JIMMY CARTER	Democratic
	Gerald R. Ford	Republican

1980	RONALD W. REAGAN	Republican
	Jimmy Carter	Democratic
	John B. Anderson	Independent
	Ed Clark	Libertarian

1984	RONALD W. REAGAN	Republican
	Walter F. Mondale	Democratic

1988	GEORGE H.W. BUSH	Republican
	Michael S. Dukakis	Democratic

1992	WILLIAM J. CLINTON	Democratic
	George H.W. Bush	Republican

FOR FURTHER READING

Books about the Presidents of the United States and their times could fill a library by themselves. They range from histories and biographies; to autobiographies, memoirs, and diaries; to collections of letters and state papers. This list is meant for those who wish to investigate further the lives of those who became President; it consists mainly of biographies, usually at least two for each person. Where the President is not mentioned in the title, the name appears in brackets following the citation.

Abrahamsen, David, *Nixon vs. Nixon: An Emotional Tragedy*, 1977.
Ambrose, Stephen E., *Eisenhower: Soldier, General of the Army, President-Elect*, 1983.
_____, *Eisenhower: The President*, 1984.
Ammon, Harry, *James Monroe: The Quest for National Identity*, 1971.
Barnard, Harry, *Rutherford B. Hayes and His America*, 1954.
Bemis, Samuel F., *John Quincy Adams and the Foundations of American Foreign Policy*, 1949.
_____, *John Quincy Adams and the Union*, 1956.
Blum, John Morton, *The Republican Roosevelt*, 1954.
_____, *Woodrow Wilson and the Politics of Morality*, 1962.
Brant, Irving, *James Madison*, 6 vols., 1941 - 1961.
Brown, Ralph A., *The Presidency of John Adams*, 1975.
Burner, David, *Herbert Hoover: A Public Life*, 1979.
Burns, James McGregor, *Roosevelt: The Lion and the Fox*, 1956.
_____, *Roosevelt: Soldier of Freedom*, 1970.
Bush, George, with Victor Gold, *Looking Forward: An Autobiography*, 1987. [Bush]

Cleaves, Freeman, *Old Tippecanoe: William Henry Harrison and His Times,* 1939.

Coles, Donald B., *Martin Van Buren and the American Political System,* 1984.

Dallek, Robert, *Ronald Reagan: The Politics of Symbolism,* 1984.

Coletta, Paolo E., *The Presidency of William Howard Taft,* 1973.

Dangerfield, George, *The Era of Good Feelings,* 1952. [Monroe]

Davison, Kenneth E., *The Presidency of Rutherford B. Hayes,* 1972.

Donovan, Robert J., *The Presidency of Harry S. Truman,* 2 vols., 1977 - 1982.

Downes, Randolph C., *The Rise of Warren Gamaliel Harding, 1865 - 1920,* 1970.

Dyer, Brainerd, *Zachary Taylor,* 1946.

Fink, Gary M., *Prelude to the Presidency,* 1980. [Carter]

Flexner, James Thomas, *George Washington,* 4 vols., 1965 - 1972.

Freeman, Douglas Southall, *George Washington,* 7 vols., 1948 - 1957.

Goebel, Dorothy B., *William Henry Harrison: A Political Biography,* 1926.

Griffis, William E., *Millard Fillmore,* 1915.

Hamilton, Holman, *Zachary Taylor,* 1941.

Harbaugh, William H., *The Life and Times of Theodore Roosevelt,* 1961.

Hargreaves, Mary, *The Presidency of John Quincy Adams,* 1985.

Hartmann, Robert T., *Palace Politics: An Inside Account of the Ford Years,* 1980.

Hesseltine, William B., *Ulysses S. Grant: Politician,* 1935.

Hoff-Wilson, Joan, *Herbert Hoover: Forgotten Progressive,* 1975.

Howe, George F., *Chester A. Arthur,* 1934.

Johnson, Haynes, *In the Absence of Power,* 1980. [Carter]

Kearns, Doris, *Lyndon Johnson and the American Dream,* 1976.

Klein, Philip S. *President James Buchanan,* 1962.

Leech, Margaret P., *In the Days of McKinley,* 1959.

_____ and Harry James Brown, *The Garfield Orbit,* 1978.

Link, Arthur S., *Woodrow Wilson and the Progressive Era, 1910 - 1917,* 1954.

Malone, Dumas, *Thomas Jefferson and His Times,* 6 vols., 1948 - 1982.

McCormac, Eugene I., *James K. Polk: A Political Biography,* 1922.

McCoy, Charles A., *Polk and the Presidency,* 1960.

McCoy, Donald R., *Calvin Coolidge: The Quiet President,* 1967.

McFeely, William S., *Grant: A Biography,* 1981.

Merrill, Horace Samuel, *Bourbon Leader: Grover Cleveland and the Democratic Party,* 1957.

Miller, Merle, *Lyndon: An Oral Biography,* 1980. [Johnson]

Miller, Nathan, *FDR: An Intimate History,* 1983.

Moore, Jim and Rick Inde, *Clinton: Young Man in a Hurry,* 1992.

Morgan, H. Wayne, *William McKinley and His America,* 1963.

Morgan, Robert J., *A Whig Embattled,* 1954. [Tyler]

Murray, Robert K., *Harding Era: Warren G. Harding and His Administration,* 1969.

Nevins, Allan, *Grover Cleveland: A Study in Courage,* 1932.

Nichols, Roy F., *Franklin Pierce: Young Hickory of the Granite Hills,* 1969.

Niven, John, *Martin Van Buren: The Romantic Age of American Politics,* 1983.

Oates, Stephen P., *With Malice Toward None: The Life of Abraham Lincoln,* 1977.

Parmet, Herbert S., *Eisenhower and the American Crusades,* 1972.

_____, *Jack: The Struggles of John F. Kennedy,* 1980.

_____, *JFK: The Presidency of John F. Kennedy,* 1983.

Peskin, Allan, *Garfield,* 1978.

Peterson, Merrill, *Thomas Jefferson and the New Nation,* 1970.

Pringle, Henry F., *The Life and Times of William Howard Taft,* 2 vols., 1939.

Rayback, Robert J., *Millard Fillmore: Biography of a President,* 1959.

Reeves, Thomas C., *Gentleman Boss,* 1975. [Arthur]

Remini, Robert V., *Andrew Jackson,* 3 vols., 1977 - 1984.

Schell, Jonathan, *The Time of Illusion,* 1976. [Nixon]

Schlesinger, Jr., Arthur, *The Age of Jackson,* 1945.

Schultz, Harold, *James Madison,* 1970.

Seager II, Robert, *And Tyler Too,* 1963.

Sefton, James E., *Andrew Johnson and the Uses of Constitutional Power,* 1980.

Sievers, Harry J. *Benjamin Harrison,* 3 vols., 1952 - 1968.

Slosser, Bob, *Reagan: Inside Out,* 1984.

Smith, Elbert B., *The Presidency of James Buchanan,* 1975.

Smith, Page, *John Adams,* 2 vols., 1962.

Thomas, Benjamin P., *Abraham Lincoln,* 1952.

Truman, Margaret, *Harry S. Truman,* 1973.

White, William Allen, *A Puritan in Babylon: The Story of Calvin Coolidge,* 1938.

Winston, Robert W., *Andrew Johnson: Plebeian and Patriot,* 1928.

INDEX

committee membership,
2:108-109
delegates, **1:**23, 53, 63; **2:**ix-x,
2.2-105; **3:**20, 27, 31, 38, 41,
55, 59, 67, 75, 105, 123;
4:28, 42, 123; **5:**1-2, 13, 17;
6:4-5, 10
nonsigning delegates, **2:**104-
107
presidency issues, **6:**1-2
president of, **2:**2-3
Constitutional Union Party,
6:99
Contee, Benjamin, **4:**44
Continental Army, **2:**24, 40, 45,
46; **4:**32; **6:**6
Continental Congresses, **3:**1-2,
132
delegates, **2:**50-51, 60-61;
3:37, 59, 72, 79, 94, 120,
123, 126; **5:**7
presidency, **1:**3; **6:**86
in 1776, **1:**122-126
Conway Cabal, **2:**40
Coolidge, Calvin, **5:**62; **6:**60-61,
96, 101
Copyright, **4:**136
Countryman Letters, **4:**28
"Court Packing" plan, **5:**60
Cox, James N., **6:**100
Crawford, William H., **6:**98
Creek Indians, **3:**42, 83-84, 123
Cresap, Michael, **2:**105
Crittenden, John, **6:**37
Cuba, **6:**33, 51, 71
Curtis, Benjamin R., **5:**85
Cushing, William, **5:**16, 22, 84
Czolgosz, Leon, **6:**51

Dalton, Tristram, **3:**13, 52-53,
92, 126, 130

Dana, Richard Henry, **1:**21
Daniel, Peter V., **5:**85
Daugherty, Henry, **6:**59
Davie, William Richardson,
2:106-107, 109
Davis, David, **5:**85
Davis, Jefferson, **6:**31
Davis, John W., **6:**101
Day, William R., **5:**86
Dayton, Elias, **2:**34
Dayton, Jonathan, **2:**34-35
Debs, Eugene V., **6:**100
Debs case, **5:**44, 48
Declaration of Independence,
3:61; **4:**1
biographies of signers, **1:**2-
113
non-signing members of
Congress, **1:**123-124
order of signing, **1:**3
physician signatories, **1:**4
preliminaries to, **1:**126-27
signers, **1:**118-21; **3:**37, 47,
120, 123, 126; **4:**27-28
text, **1:**114-17
Declaration of Rights (Virginia), **4:**19, 143-144, 145
*Defense of the Constitutions of
the United States of America* (Adams), **6:**7
De Lancey family, **2:**28-29;
3:107, 108
Delaware, **1:**66-67, 68-69, 70-71,
122; **2:**56-57, 58-59, 60-61,
62-63, 64-65, 111; **3:**34-35,
36-38, 130; **4:**4-5, 8, 36, 144
Delian League, **3:**1
Democratic Party, **5:**27, 28;
6:19, 21, 25, 30, 33, 35, 37,
57, 67, 71, 73, 79, 85, 90,
91, 98, 99, 100, 101, 102
Democratic-Republican Party,